Hélène Seckel

Musée Picasso

Visitor's Guide

Réunion
des Musées
Nationaux

View of Room 8, Ground Floor

Cover: *The Bathers*, 1918, (detail)

ISBN 2-7118-3532-4

© Editions de la Réunion des musées nationaux
  49, rue Etienne-Marcel, 75001 Paris
© Succession Picasso, 1996

The History of a Collection

The Picassos of Picasso

"I am the greatest collector of Picassos in the world." Only one person could have said these words, and that person is none other than Picasso himself. Indeed, throughout his long career as an artist, he accumulated and held onto a large number of his own works, which he kept stacked away among the incredible disorder of his many studios. These works ranged from sketchbooks to the most finished masterpieces, some of which he refused to give up even in the face of the most insistent bidders, either because he was attached to them for sentimental reasons (portraits of the women in his life or of his children), or because he considered them to be major works from which he could not part and which he liked to have close at hand. Such was the precious collection that he left behind at the time of his death in 1973.

1979, The dation

In 1968, a law was enacted permitting heirs to pay their inheritance taxes with works of art instead of money, provided, of course, that the works could be considered as important contributions to the French cultural heritage. This is what is known as a *dation*. Applied usually as an exceptional measure, it was an obvious recourse in the case of the Picasso estate. Dominique Bozo, a curator of the national museums, was appointed to choose from among the considerable of works that Picasso had assembled – paintings, sculptures, drawings, prints, ceramics, illustrated books – those that were to constitute the dation. He submitted his selection to Jean Leymarie, a personal friend of the artist and the organizer of the retrospective exhibition "Hommage à Picasso", held in Paris in 1966. Officially ratified in 1979, the selection that was to result in the creation of this museum included works from all periods and in all techniques; highly finished museum pieces, but also coherent series of studies (such as the drawings and sketchbooks leading to the *Demoiselles d'Avignon),* as well as works of a more experimental and intimate nature (such as the small Cubist constructions), for a total of 203 paintings, 158 sculptures (the dation's strongest collection, and the only one of its kind), 29 "relief-pictures", 88 ceramic pieces, some

View of Room 16, Lower Level

paper collages, about 1,500 drawings, some thirty sketchbooks, and more than 1,600 prints. Certain periods are extremely well represented (in particular the Twenties and Thirties), while others less so (especially the Blue and Rose periods).

The *Donation Picasso:* his personal collection

In addition to works by Picasso himself, the museum owns works by other artists that he had collected (Braque, Cézanne, Degas, Rousseau, Matisse...) and that he had hoped would someday become a public collection. His wish became reality when his heirs agreed upon the donation of some fifty works of art from his personal collection in 1978; which would first be exhibited in the Louvre. The dation completed the donation with works by De Chirico and Seurat, Iberian bronzes and, above all, examples of primitive art.

Recent acquisitions

The collections of the museum have also been enriched by acquisitions; through purchases (*Composition with a Butterfly,* 1932, *Portrait of Guillaume Apollinaire Wounded,* 1916), bequests (*Still Life with a Razor Strap,* 1909, bequeathed by Daniel-Henry Kahnweiler), or gifts, and in particular one of the great paintings of the Blue Period, the *Celestina* from 1904, donated by Fredrik Roos in 1990; a sculpture, the Woman *Brushing Her Hair*, 1906, given by Georges Pellequer and Philippe Colas; the *Three Figures Under a Tree* from 1906-1907, one of prize paintings of the Douglas Cooper collection, given in 1986 by his heir, William McCarty-Cooper; the complete series of "bons à tirer" (final proofs) for the one hundred prints that constitute the *Suite Vollard,* given by Roger and Madeleine Lacourière. In keeping with the exceptional nature of this event – the creation of this museum –, the artist's heirs approved the execution of a large-scale version of one of the maquettes proposed in 1928 as a project for a monument to Guillaume Apollinaire (this was justified by the fact that Picasso in his lifetime had approved a large-scale version of the other maquette for the Museum of Modern Art in New York). These collections have been further enriched by the acquisition of illustrated books and archives (Picasso's letters to Guillaume Apollinaire).

1990, a new dation
Jacqueline Picasso, the artist's widow, died tragically in 1986. Her daughter offered a new dation composed of 47 paintings (a group particularly rich in works from the painter's last years), 2 sculptures, about forty drawings, and an important series of 24 sketchbooks, many previously unknown, along with engravings and ceramic works. This new set of works will benefit not only the Musée Picasso, but about twenty other museums throughout France.

Permanent loans
In order to fill chronological gaps and to balance its collections, the Musée Picasso effected certain exchanges with the Musée National d'Art Moderne. On permanent loan to the Musée Picasso, therefore, are a few noteworthy works such as the *Portrait of Gustave Coquiot* (1901) and a *Seated Nude* from 1905, as well as one or the other of the works given to the French state by Michel and Louise Leiris in 1984, like the famous 1914 sculpture *The Absinth Glass.*

The Musée Picasso

History of the Hôtel Salé
The mansion which has become the home of the new Musée Picasso was built between 1656 and 1659 for Pierre Aubert, Lord of Fontenay, who had amassed a considerable fortune as a collector of the Salt Tax. This is why the Hôtel Aubert de Fontenay was ironically nicknamed by contemporaries the "hôtel Salé" (which means "salted" in French). The architect was Jean Boullier, also called Jean de Bourges, about whom very little is known. With its impressive size, its sumptuous appearance, its clearly ordered architecture, and the quality of its decoration, it ranks among the finest historic houses of the Marais. The large portal facing the rue de Thorigny opens onto a semi-circular forecourt bordered, on the right, by the former service wing whose presence explains the off-center composition of the façade, which is crowned by a monumental arched pediment (the façade on the garden side is flanked by two protruding pavilions and is perfectly symmetrical). Overlooking the courtyard of the outbuildings, there is a chapel that juts out strangely from the façade at the first floor level.

The vestibule at the entrance opens onto a sumptuous grand staircase, lavishly decorated with sculptures executed by a number of artists: the two Marsy brothers, Gaspard (1624-1681) and Balthasar (1628-1674), who also worked on the sculpted decoration at Versailles; and a young sculptor who was barely twenty years old at the time, Martin Desjardins (born in Breda in 1640). On the first-floor landing, three large arches lead to the Salon de Jupiter, which is decorated with statues of this god and of Juno. The interlaced monograms of Pierre Aubert and his wife Marie Chastelain are a ubiquitous feature of the decoration, which is completed by a magnificent wrought-iron balustrade. The ground floor and the first floor consist of a series of large rooms that face either the garden or the front court; the spacious, interconnecting salons on the first floor overlooking the garden are particularly impressive because of their majestic proportions. The attic storey on the second floor is occupied by smaller rooms. A vaulted cellar runs under the entire building.

Over the centuries, the Hôtel Salé changed hands many times, either through sale or inheritance, and saw a variety of occupants: in 1671, it was rented to the embassy of the Republic of Venice, and in 1688 to the Maréchal de Villeroy, who was followed by a series of other tenants; then, in 1768, the daughter of the owner at the time used it as dowry for her marriage to the Marquis de Juigné, after which it became known as the Hôtel de Juigné; during the Revolution, it was expropriated by the State; in 1815 it became an educational establishment (in which Balzac finished his schooling and which he later wrote about in *Les Petits Bourgeois*).

Between 1829 and 1884, it housed the Ecole Centrale des Arts et Manufactures, which brought about considerable modifications in the buildings in order to accommodate its various facilities: laboratories, amphitheaters, offices, libraries, study halls, as well as an apartment for the director. Afterwards, it was unoccupied for a few years (part of the interior decoration was placed in storage; in particular the panels painted by Desportes and Coypel above the doors). In 1887, it was rented by the bronzesmith Vian, who had the mansion partially restored and who used its salons to display the products from his foundry. Starting in 1943, the buildings housed the municipal Ecole des Métiers d'Art. In 1964, and by then in a fairly dilapidated state, the Hôtel Salé was acquired by the City of Paris, but only in 1968 was it finally granted the status of a historical monument. After a few emergency repairs, a program of restoration was conducted from 1974 until 1980 under the direction of the architects Bernard Vitry and Bernard Fonquernie of the Monuments Historiques.

The installation of the museum
The choice of this site for the Musée Picasso, supported by the Secretary of State for Culture, Michel Guy, was not without its opponents, although Picasso himself, who had always chosen to live in old houses, would probably have been delighted. Once it had been decided upon, a competition was held to determine who would design the museum's facilities. The project of the architect Roland Simounet was selected in 1976 from among the four that were submitted; the others were by Roland Castro and the G.A.U. (Groupement pour l'Architecture et l'Urbanisme), Jean Monge, and Carlo Scarpa. The problem was how to adapt a 17th-century private mansion to the needs of a modern museum open to a large pu-

View of Room 6, First Floor

blic (organization of the visit through the collections, conception of a presentation in harmony with the site, solution of the technical problems involved in the display of works of art: lighting, temperature, security) all the while preserving its architectural integrity. By and large, the interior, which had received considerable modifications (subdivision of levels and rooms), has been restored to its former state, restituting the original disposition of the volumes and their noble proportions.

Assistance in the refurbishing of the interior was provided by the Mobilier National, which entrusted an artist with the execution of certain elements of the decoration; the lanterns and candelabras of the grand staircase, the chandeliers in the vestibule and in the salons of the first floor, and the furnishings of the rooms (seats, chairs, tables) were designed especially for the museum by Diego Giacometti.

The itinerary of the visit through the museum was dictated by the architecture: the grand staircase very naturally draws visitors up to the first floor to begin the tour of the permanent collections, displayed in the interconnecting salons overlooking the garden; at the end of this series of rooms, there are stairs leading back to the ground floor, where the visit continues with the sculpture garden, located in the courtyard of the old stables, which is now covered with a skylight; from there, ramps lead through the lower level back to the ground floor and to the garden, where a few sculptures are displayed. Except for a few rooms with thematic presentations, the visit follows a chronological sequence, and, in accordance with the constant dialogue that existed between the different mediums in which Picasso worked, paintings, drawings, sculptures, and prints are all displayed together. Documents of various kinds (photographs, manuscripts, newspaper clippings, magazines) are also on display to provide additional information on each period.

On the second floor, a special area has been set aside for the display of part of the *Donation Picasso*, for prints and for temporary exhibitions. Located on the third floor are the library, the documentation and archives department (reserved for research), and the offices of the curators. Access to the reception area and the bookshop located in the former caretaker's lodge may be gained through the courtyard.

Note

This guide presents a room-by-room visit through the permanent collections. The display of the works may, however, be subject to modification: it can happen that a work described as being displayed in a certain room will have been moved to another one, or even temporarily withdrawn from display, either for loan to another exhibition or for technical reasons.

Due to their fragility, drawings and prints cannot be displayed for extended lengths of time, and so will be presented on a rotating basis.

Preceding each article on the works listed in this guide are the title, date, and place of execution (in brackets if uncertain).

Unless otherwise indicated, the works belong to the 1979 dation.

In the captions, the dimensions are given in the following order: height x width x depth.

Room 1

The Early Years
The Blue Period

1881-1903

1881	October 25	Pablo Ruiz Picasso born in Málaga, the son of José Ruiz Blasco, a painter and drawing professor, and Maria Picasso y Lasis.
1891		Appointment of Picasso's father to a teaching position in La Coru Blasco, a painter and drawing professor, an
1895	Summer	Move to Barcelona, where Don José has a new position at the School of Fine Arts, La Lonja; Picasso admitted to attend the advanced classes that autumn.
1899		In Barcelona, Picasso frequents the Els Quatre Gats café, a fashionable meeting place for the literary and artistic avant-garde.
1900	October	Picasso makes a trip to Paris with his friend Casagemas, returning to Spain by Christmas.
1901	May	Second trip to Paris, where he stays until the end of the year and meets Max Jacob.
	Autumn	Beginning of the Blue Period.
1902	October	Third trip to Paris, where Picasso undergoes difficult times.

Picasso at the age
of seven with his sister Lola
(Archives Picasso)

14

The Barefoot Girl

Early 1895, La CorutriPicasso's first works display a positively amazing skill (he would later say that he never made any children's drawings, that at the age of twelve he drew like Raphael). He was only fourteen – scarcely older than his model – when he painted this sad-faced, weary, and slightly sullen street-urchin. Certain features of this portrait are striking for their unconventionality; deliberately stressed, certain details take on a particular importance: the bare feet ("the children of the poor in our country always went about barefoot, and this little girl's feet were covered with sores," Picasso later recalled), the large, ungainly hands, the unsymmetric features of the face, with one cheek puffier than the other, and the slightly cross-eyed gaze of the very dissimilar eyes. At the time, Picasso still signed his works: P. Ruiz.

The Barefoot Girl
Oil on canvas
75 x 50 cm

The Death of Casagemas
Oil on wood
27 x 35 cm

The Death of Casagemas

Summer 1901,
Paris

Casagemas, the Barcelona painter and friend with whom Picasso had made his first trip to Paris, committed suicide over an unhappy love affair at the beginning of 1901. A few months later, as if to exorcise this death (which must have haunted him all the more because he had moved into his friend's studio on the Boulevard de Clichy), Picasso painted several portraits of the suicide, whom we see here lying in state, in a profile view, with the blackened hole of the fatal wound still visible on his temple. The candle flame – a symbol of the fragility of life – radiates a strange polychrome glow (long brushstrokes of pure color, a technique reminiscent of Van Gogh), casting a golden highlight on the dead man's profile. This was the period which saw the appearance of the blue color-schemes that characterized Picasso's work between 1901 and 1904: "It was with the death of Casagemas in mind that I began to paint in blue."

Portrait of Gustave Coquiot

1901,
Paris
(On permanent loan from
the Musée National d'Art Moderne,
gift of Mme. Coquiot, 1933).

In June 1901, there was a large exhibition of Picasso's works at Ambroise Vollard's gallery on rue Laffitte (it was on this occasion that the painter met the poet Max Jacob). The organizers of the exhibition were Pere Manyac – a Catalan living in Paris and Picasso's dealer – and the critic Gustave Coquiot; the latter described the young Spaniard as a "frenzied lover of modern life," an impression confirmed by his works: portraits, street and park scenes, cabaret interiors and bordellos; works brimming with virtuosity and violent colors, in an expressionistic manner akin to that of Steinlen, Lautrec, and Munch. In this portrait of the critic, we see a massive and complacent figure, probably in a cabaret setting (with scantily clad dancers wriggling in the back-

ground); the very red mouth with its broad smile stands out against the starkly lit face. The paint was laid on thickly, with broad brushstrokes. The artist had chosen by then to sign his works with his mother's name: Picasso.

Self-Portrait

Late 1901,
Paris

By the end of 1901, the monochrome blue color-schemes had become an established feature of Picasso's work and would continue to be so until 1904, giving rise to what has justifiably come to be known as his "Blue Period". This color, chosen for its expressivity, allowed him to go beyond realistic representation: the color of sadness – "Picasso believes that life is based on suffering," Sabartés wrote – here accentuates the dismay expressed in the artist's emaciated features and joyless gaze; who would

Portrait of Gustave Coquiot
Oil on canvas
100 x 80 cm

Self-Portrait
Oil on canvas
81 x 60 cm

Celestina
Oil on canvas
70 x 56 cm

Room 1

guess this to be the portrait of a young man of twenty? Charles Morice, art critic and friend of Gauguin, spoke then of "the amazingly sterile sadness" that overshadowed the work of Picasso, "that frighteningly precocious child".

Celestina

March 1904,
Barcelona
Gift of Fredrik Roos, 1989

Picasso painted this portrait probably very shortly before definitively leaving Barcelona for Paris in April 1904. It shows an old woman whose gaze is deformed by a leucoma of the left eye. The shapeless black cloak that enshrouds her body sets off by contrast the very realistically rendered face: the greyish hair covered with a lace mantilla, the cheeks somewhat hollowed by age, the corners of the mouth and chin covered with unbecoming hairs, and the sagging flesh of the neck. In this, one of the last works of the famous Blue Period, the monochrome blue color-scheme is barely lightened by the rosy tints of the cheeks and the nacreous touch of the earring, which gives an uncanny feeling to this figure set against an indefinite background, staring into space, just over the spectator's right shoulder, with the skewed gaze of her single eye.

The figure portrayed is Carlotta Valdivia, said to have been a procuress. In any case, the picture is called la Celestina, a name given to procuresses after the character of the same name in Fernando de Rojas's *La Tragicomedia de Calisto e Melibea* (1499) who sells the chaste Melibea's favors to the passionate Calisto.

Room 2   From the Rose Period to the Demoiselles d'Avignon

1904-1907

1904	April	Picasso returns to Paris (he will remainin France from then on, making only occasional trips abroad) and takes a studio at the Ba-teau-Lavoir, in Montmartre (a picturesque but squalid wooden structure on Place Ravignan - today Place Emile-Goudeau - which was unfortunately destroyed by fire in 1970).
	Autumn	He meets Fernande Olivier, who will be his companion until the spring of 1912.
1905	Beginning of the year	Beginning of the Rose Period. Picasso meets the poet Guillaume Apollinaire.
	Autumn	Exhibition of Ingres's *Turkish Bath* at the salon d'Automne. Picasso meets Gertrude Stein.
	Winter	Presentation at the Louvre of 5th-3rd century BC Iberian sculpture found in excavations at Osuna and Cerro de Los Santo, in the south of Spain.
1906	Spring	Picasso meets Matisse.
	Summer	Trip to Gosol, a Catalan village near Andorra.
	October	Death of Cézanne: several exhibitions of his works over the following year.
1907	Spring	Picasso meets Braque.
	March-July	Work on *Les Demoiselles d'Avignon*.
	June	A visit to the Museum of Ethnography at Trocadero brings to Picasso the "revelation" of African Art.

Fernande Olivier,
Picasso, and Ram,
the art ofin Barcelona in 1906
(Archives Picasso, photo:
Vidal Ventosa)

Seated Nude
Oil on cardboard
106 x 76 cm

The Jester
Bronze
41.5 x 37 x 22.8 cm

Seated Nude

1905,
Paris
(On permanent loan from the Musée
National d'Art Moderne, acquired 1954)

Picasso progressively abandoned the blue color-schemes in favor of grey, ocher, and rose tonalities. With its blue and rose colors, this nude is a transitional work between Picasso's Blue Period and what has come to be called his Rose Period. The handling of the slender, almost sickly, model is still in the manneristic vein of the figures of the blue paintings. The pallid rose of the fine-featured, thin-lipped face, and disproportionately long-fingered hand stands out against the dark gray-blue of the background and the bistre-colored cardboard support. This painting once belonged to Gertrude Stein, the American writer who, along with her brothers Leo and Michael, established herself in Paris at the beginning of the century. The Steins befriended many painters and assembled impressive collections of pain-

tings. Michael championed Matisse, while Gertrude and Leo became enthusiastic supporters of Picasso.

The Jester

1905,
Paris

The beginning of 1905 saw the appearance of a new theme in Picasso's work: the saltimbanques. The painter was fascinated by the melancholy and rootless world of itinerant performers – so dear to Guillaume Apollinaire – with its population of lithe-bodied acrobats, equestriennes, jugglers, multicolored Harlequins and other players of the commedia dell'arte. Although the museum has no paintings representative of this period in its collections, it does own many drawings, and this bust of a buffoon wearing a fool's cap and smiling an ambiguous smile. After one of his many evenings spent at the Médrano circus, at the foot of

Montmartre, Picasso started to execute a bust of his friend the poet Max Jacob, but ended up modifying the head to represent a clown figure (only the lower part of the face retains the poet's features).

Three Dutch Girls

Summer 1905,
Schoorl
(On permanent loan from the Musée National d'Art Moderne, donated by André and Jeanne Lefèvre, 1961)

During the summer of 1905, Picasso made a trip to Holland upon the invitation of a writer friend, and returned to Paris with some works that were quite different from his previous ones. Here, we see three full and healthy-bodied Dutch girls (Picasso did make fun of them somewhat, finding they had "waists like cuirassiers"), standing with their feet planted firmly on the ground, their bellies thrust forward, rather devoid of elegance, it is true, even though they form the traditional group of the three

Graces. The flat landscape setting showing the thatched roofs of the Alkneaar region has been rendered in an picturesque way by a strange transparent color-scheme that hints at the moistness of the atmosphere.

Head of a Woman (Fernande)

1906,
Paris

In the autumn of 1904, Picasso made the acquaintance of another of his neighbors at the Bateau-Lavoir, a young woman named Fernande Olivier, with whom he set up house after a year. Hers was an impressive and calm beauty, and she became the subject of a series of works, mostly paintings, which express the sensual nature of her relationship with the painter. On one side of this sculpted head we see Fernande's handsome profile, with its finely drawn eyebrow, almond-shaped eye, high cheekbone, slightly arched nose, and full lips about to smile, while the other side is sketchy, barely distinguishable from the mass:

Head of a Woman (Fernande)
Bronze
35 x 24 x 25 cm

Three Dutch Girls
Gouache on paper
77 x 67 cm

Room 2

the eye has been summarily incised in the rough clay (the plasticity of the original medium has been well rendered by the bronze cast), in an effort at simplification, using less means for greater expressivity.

The Two Brothers

Summer 1906,
Gosol

Although this nude figure of a young boy carrying his little brother is reminiscent of the saltimbanques of 1905 (the drum on the ground is a circus accessory), it is a far cry from the emaciated acrobats of before, and farther still from the stricken figures of the Blue Period. Here, on the contrary, the body of the young boy proudly displays its nudity brimming with health, its frame and muscles firm and nicely rounded. Unlike the flat silhouettes of the year before, these figures have been given volume, and are modelled in the rose tints of a healthy skin-coloring. The attitude of the main figure,

which recalls archaic Greek statuary, contributes to the impression of stability. This painting displays the characteristics of the works executed at Gosol, both as to its theme - nude figures, the serene and bucolic setting of a former age - and its handling - solidity of the forms, accentuation of the volumes and the palette of rose, ocher and grey tones that are the selfsame earth colors as those of this village perched in the hills of Catalonia, where in many respects Picasso effected a return to his sources. It is interesting to note that Picasso persisted in using monochrome color-schemes at the very time that the dominant tendency - Fauvism - favored the all-out use of color.

Bust of a Woman (Fernande)

Summer 1906,
Gosol

In all likelihood, the features of the finely-shaped face sculpted at the top of this large piece of wood are those of Fernande. It is

The Two Brothers
Gouache on cardboard
80 x 59 cm

Bust of a Woman (Fernande)
Sculpted boxwood
77 x 15.5 x 15 cm

surprising to note the disproportion in the degree of detail between the head and the body. Apparently this work is unfinished: black outlines painted on the wood indicate summarily the arms and chest of a full-length female figure (this is confirmed by certain drawings in the sketchbook used by Picasso during his stay in Gosol, the "Catalan sketchbook", which show the whole figure). The unfinished aspect probably pleased Picasso, who often used this effect in his sculptures.

Woman Dressing Her Hair

1906,
Paris
(Gift of Georges Pellequer
and Philippe Colas, 1981)

Simplification and stylization have continued to progress since the preceding year: in this work, which is related to other paintings and drawings, the figure of the woman has been gathered into a compact form encompassed by the hair flowing down her left side. The face has been treated summarily and displays some of the cha-

Woman Dressing Her Hair
Bronze
42.2 x 26 x 31.8 cm

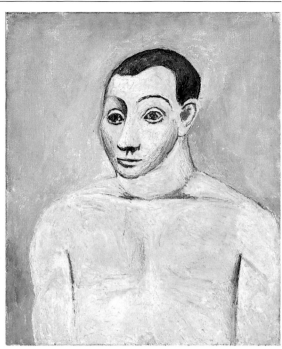

Self-Portrait
Oil on canvas
65 x 54 cm

racteristics of the antique Iberian sculpture that was then being exhibited at the Louvre: prominence of the ears and especially of the blank eye, which is capped by equally protuberant eyelids and brow. The theme of the "coiffure" – a woman combing her hair or having it combed – was probably inspired by Ingres's *Turkish Bath* that Picasso had seen the previous year at the Salon d'Automne; the woman's morphology, round belly and heavy thighs, is indeed reminiscent of Ingres's bathers.

Self-Portrait

Autumn 1906,
Paris

As in the blue self-portrait of 1901, the painter seems to be emerging from the empty space of a uniform background. What is striking here is the rough simplification used by Picasso; the result of his work in Gosol and the fruit of his study of Iberian art was a new kind of figuration that was already at quite a remove from reality. The choice of certain expressive, sty-lized elements, divorced from any realism or ideal representation, allowed him to stress the essentials: the tenacity of a gaze, the solidity of the body. The face has become a mask: its shape reduced to an oval, the eyes as black dots under heavy lids (perhaps influenced by Catalan Romanesque painting), and the ears greatly enlarged. The head rests strangely on a cylindrical neck (could this be a reference to the art of Cézanne, which presented a certain geometrization of forms?), itself connected to a large bust whose anatomy is strongly structured by the horizontal axis of the collarbones and the verticals that define the torso.

Rooms **2-3** Studies for *Les Demoiselles d'Avignon* Wood Sculptures of 1907-1908 Picasso and Primitive Art

Studies for *Les Demoiselles d'Avignon*

1907

Since 1939 this famous painting has been in the collections of the Museum of Modern Art in New York. As for the Musée Picasso, it owns several painted studies, a great number of drawings and, especially, seven sketchbooks that help us to understand the creation of the *Demoiselles d'Avignon*.

What is it about? The nude women are prostitutes in a bordello of the rue d'Avignon in Barcelona who are receiving their clients; seated among them are a sailor and a medical student (a *"carabin"*, in French slang). Several studies for the various figures are on display here: a seated woman whose face presents some characteristic features of Iberian art, a simplification of the forms, as well as a stylization which ac-

centuates certain details through formal amplifications (blank eyes, huge ears, face reduced to an oval: elements that Picasso had been able to study on two sculpted Iberian heads that he had just bought - not realizing that they had been stolen from the Louvre!); a bust shows us the figure of the sailor, who is dressed in the traditional uniform: the facial features have been brutally simplified, the shadow areas in this otherwise flat representation have been rendered as hatchmarks; yet other figures have been stylized even to the point of dif-

Head of a Sailor
Paris, Spring 1907
Oil on cardboard
53.5 x 36.2 cm

Les Demoiselles d'Avignon, Paris, May-July 1907
Oil on canvas, 243.9 x 233.7 cm
New York, The Museum of Modern Art

Seated Nude
Paris Winter 1906-1907
Oil on canvas
121 x 93.5 cm

formity, such as that of the *Bust of a Woman with Large Ear*, underneath which can be seen (not very easily with the naked eye, but very clearly on laboratory documents) one of the steps in the composition of the painting. In fact, in the final version, the anecdote has disappeared: there is no more sailor, no more medical student; only five female nudes intensely returning the spectator's gaze.

All of these studies serve to throw light on what Picasso had in mind and how he proceeded: responding to a certain number of models (Ingres's *Turkish Bath,* Cézanne's *Bathers)* and reacting to the solutions found by Matisse, he set out to paint a picture that would solve in a new way the pictorial problem in question: how to represent figures in space without resorting to the traditional means of illusionism (the appearance of depth and volume being created through linear perspective and the play of light and shade). Picasso did not hesitate to distort the human figure, chopping it up into fragments and scattering them, or to

Bust of a Woman with Large Ear
(photo by the Laboratoire des Musées
de France which shows a compositional
study of the five figures for the
Demoiselles d'Avignon underneath).

Figure
Sculpted boxwood
35.2 x 12.2 x 12 cm

Figure
Sculpted oak
80.5 x 24 x 20.8 cm

Head of a Man
Carved beech
37 x 20 x 12 cm
1990 Dation

disfigure it, representing, for example, a face in frontal view but with the nose as a flat profile (ironically described by some as a "slice of Brie"), which procedure must have disconcerted, if not shocked, even his closest friends at the time.

Wood Sculptures of 1907-1908

The archaism which frequently appears in Picasso's work starting in 1906 manifests itself here in the very choice of the technique that he used to carve a series of sculptures in 1907 and 1908 (the wood being worked with a sharp instrument). There is something outdated about this way of working the wood (practically only Gauguin had used it, and his work had been well represented at the Salon d'Automne of 1906, an obvious inspiration for Picasso), which gives rise to a certain brutality in the handling of the figures. In all likelihood, when Picasso carved these various pieces, he had already seen works of primitive African or Oceanian art (Matisse had shown him some at the

end of 1906 and Picasso had discovered the collections of the Museum of Ethnography at Trocadero at the beginning of the summer of 1907). Some of the sculptures that have been roughly shaped looked like totems: the *Standing Nude* smeared with yellow paint, or the impressive *Figure*, whose massive forms have barely been freed from

Three Nudes
Carved beech
32 x 15,4 x 3,2 cm

the block from which it was carved; the latter resembles the Tiki from the Marquesas Islands that Picasso owned (standing figure, legs slightly bent, elbows close to the body and fists clenched in front of the chest) with rather simian features drawn with red and white paint. The 1907 *Head of a Man* – which is an extremely primitivistic interpretation of one of the Iberian sculptures stolen from the Louvre by Guillaume Apollinaire's secretary and which Picasso kept for four years before returning it in 1911 - is directly related to the major painting of the same year, *Les Demoiselles d'Avignon*. Other sculptures are more refined, for example the *Figure* (whose ears recall the hairstyle of the Lady of Elch, a famous Iberian sculpture whose authenticity is contested today) or the *Three Nudes,* which have been inscribed in the round form of what may originally have been a washboard.

Picasso and Primitive Art

At the beginning of the century, art objects from Africa and Oceania could be found at the flea market, in curiosity shops, or at certain art dealers who were already specialized in "Negro art". These objects interested artists such as Derain, Matisse, and Vlaminck, who collected them; Picasso himself had a collection of primitive objects which he assembled all through his life. It is an established fact that some of these objects, today in the museum's collections, were acquired at the beginning stages of the Cubist experiment: for example, the two roof posts in the shape of a man and a woman from New Caledonia that can be seen in a photograph of Picasso's studio taken in 1908, or the little Punu mask whitened with kaolin from Gabon visible in a 1911 photograph. More examples of Picasso's taste for primitive art, which he saw with eyes other than those of an ethnographer or a connoisseur, will be encountered farther on in the tour: a mask with bulging cylindrical

Two wooden figures
from New Caledonia on the wall
of the studio at the Bateau-Lavoir
Paris, 1908
(Documentation du musée Picasso,
photo: G. Burgess)

Ceremonial headdress:
Nevinbumbaau
New Hebrides

eyes from the Grebo tribe of the Ivory coast (given to the museum by Marina Ruiz-Picasso in 1983), a mask from the Nimba tribe of Guinea (which Picasso had in 1931 at Boisgeloup, and which may have influenced his work on the great sculpted heads of that year); a bronze head from Benin (acquired in 1944); or that disquieting, brightly colored figure from the New Hebrides given to him by Matisse, calling it "a magical, terribly wild sculpture". Which was Picasso's feeling about primitive art in general, for he saw in it the work of sorcerers who tamed spirits by giving them form. It was not so much a matter of influence as one of a convergence of the primitive mode of representation and the trajectory of Picasso's art: the idea behind these African forms (to represent what is "known" about an object, rather than what is "seen", which will be one of the main points of Cubism) was every bit as important to him as their appearance (dictated by rules of representation that were different from those of Western art).

Room 3

From *Les Demoiselles d'Avignon* to the "Cézannian" phase of Cubism

1907-1909

1907	Summer	The first visit by a young art dealer named Daniel-Henry Kahnweiler to Picasso's studio marks the beginning of a lifelong association and friendship.
1908		Picasso's painting bears distinct traces of Cézanne's influence (geometrization of the forms, accentuation of the modelling of the volumes).
	Summer	Stays at La Rue-des-Bois, near Creil, in the Oise district.
	September	Picasso and Braque, who had met the year before, begin to work in close association.
	November	Braque exhibition at Kahnweiler's gallery. The critic Louis Vauxcelles wrote on this occasion: "He reduces everything to geometric patterns, or cubes", hence the origin of the term Cubism.

Daniel-Henry Kahnweiler
in Picasso's studio,
11, boulevard de Clichy,
Paris,
Autumn 1910
(Archives Picasso)

Mother and Child
Oil on canvas
81 x 60 cm

Mother and Child

Summer 1907,
Paris

The theme of motherhood may well have been close to Picasso's heart, but this did not prevent him from disfiguring it. How not to feel aggressed by the brightness of the colors, the violence of the extreme contrast between the red and the green? The great simplification of the forms, the flat areas that seem to have been cut out directly from the colors and assembled on the canvas, make for a very schematic picture, one that is peculiarly wild and atavistic in its awkwardness. We get the same impression from the drawing of the faces: the eyes are uneven, the nose has been reduced to a simple line bordered with hatching as if to indicate relief. Here there is no doubt as to the influence of Negro art, which Picasso had discovered at the Museum of Ethnography at the Trocadero early in the summer of 1907, and in particular that of the ritual scarification that appears on certain Africain masks. But on the masks the scars are symmetrical, they are elements of balance; whereas here, the hatching reinforces the impression of dissymmetry and disequilibrium. Picasso has used these conventional forms in his own way and towards his own ends: to express the impression made on him by these tribal masks and their sacred and disquieting wildness born of a world of magic.

Three Figures Under a Tree
Oil on canvas
99 x 99 cm

Room 3

Reclining Nude and Three Figures
Oil on wood
36 x 62 cm

Three Figures Under a Tree

Autumn 1907,
Paris
Gift of William McCarty-Cooper

Three masks. The three faces are handled in the same anonymous and expressionless manner: geometric ovals for the face, hollow eye-sockets, noses like wooden wedges. The influence of Negro art is generally evoked in connection with this type of picture, especially because of the impersonal aspect of the figures and the rough stylization which gives them the appearance of carved wood. The torsos also have an identical handling: the broad curved line of the shoulders is repeated three times in the curves of the breasts. At the bottom of the picture, the forms are more confusing: it is not always possible to tell which parts of the three joined bodies are represented by the curvilinear motifs, which seem mostly to help articulate the pictorial surface. Note the economy of the means, but also the ambiguous representation which results: a single line may serve twice, defining for example the forehead of one of the figures and the cheek of the other, the arm of one and the outline of the torso of another. The entire canvas, from the tree above to the light areas at the bottom - which may represent towels or clothing - is completely occupied and composed of a rhythmic sequence of surfaces of fairly equal size. The unity of the whole, due to this compact and regularly ordered formal coherence, is further reinforced by the color-scheme: the figures and the background are handled in

an identical fashion. The thin layer of paint occupies each of the areas defined by broad black outlines. It was generally reworked with hatched lines of a greater thickness, the darkest of which define the shadows. The restrained green, blue, ocher and brown color-scheme will characterize the Cubist works of the following year. The geometrization of the forms, the overall occupation of the pictorial surface, and the blending of figures and ground, are the first signs of the new style to come.

Reclining Nude and Three Figures

Spring 1908,
Paris

Judging by the disposition of the figures, this picture is yet another evocation, like the *Demoiselles d'Avignon*, of Ingres's *Turkish Bath*. It is also an allusion to Manet's *Olympia*, and more specifically to Cézanne's interpretation of this painting. The size of the reclining nude, as compared to that of the seated figure drawing a curtain aside to unveil her, tells us that she is indeed lying down (for there is no perspective construction of the kind that may be seen in a painting like Mantegna's famous *Dead Christ*), and what's more, on a surface - a white sheet - that is tilted up towards the picture plane. This reminds us naturally of the white tablecloths painted by Cézanne in compositions where the table-top appears to be almost parallel to the picture plane.

The wild colors of late 1907 have given way here to a more restrained color-scheme consisting of brown, blue and white. This painting may be seen in its original dimensions thanks to the restoration of a section on the right that had been cut away - no one knows when or why (the edges of the cut are quite apparent in the reproduction of this picture in the 1942 volume of the *Complete Works of Picasso* published by Christian Zervos).

Landscape with Two Figures

Autumn 1908,
[Paris]

The two nude figures in a landscape are an obvious allusion to the bathers of Cézanne, as is also the composition, which is structured by the lines of the tree branches that arch to frame a view of the landscape beyond. The figures are so well integrated into the forms and rhythms of the landscape that, at first glance, they may escape notice altogether. But, if this type of work has been put under the heading of "Cézannian" Cubism (the term that has come to designate the works of 1908-1909), it is for another reason: Cézanne said that "nature should be rendered as cylinders, spheres, cones, and the whole put into perspective";

accordingly, in the center of the painting there is a mass of very strongly modelled geometric volumes - most likely rocks - that have not been set off by outlines, but that have been built up only with colors that seem to be giving off their own light, an effect that Cézanne had also strived to achieve.

Still Life with a Razor Strap

1909,
Paris
(D-H. Kahnweiler Bequest, 1980).

The reference to Cézanne here consists in the use of a specific technique known as the *"passage"*, whereby forms are built up out of small planes of color that have no definite contours, but that tend to "run" into one another to create the vibrational impression of light (which is reinforced by the use of small brush strokes). The books, the fruit (plums and bananas), the basket with a festooned border on the white table-cloth, and the leather strap for the sharpening of straight-razors that is hanging and projecting its shadow on the wall, are all recognizable in this still life, in spite of the considerable geometrization of their forms, which shows that Cubism adhered to realism (certain Cubist works did verge on

Landscape with Two Figures
Oil on canvas
60 x 73 cm

Room 3

Still Life with a Razor strap
Oil on canvas
55 x 40.5 cm

abstraction, but Picasso avoided pursuing this direction so as not to fall into the trap of a purely ornamental art). The color-scheme is very simple: it consists of the grey and brown tones that were to become the characteristic colors of Cubism. The idea was to use arbitrary colors for objects instead of local colors (their so-called real color), so as to circumvent the painter's all-too subjective judgments in this area.

Room 4 The Climactic Years of Cubism

1909-1917

1909	Summer	Trip to Horta de Ebro in Spain. Picasso continues to work in the Cézannian mode, progressing in the fragmentation of forms into facets; the objects are easily recognizable.
	September	Picasso moves to 11, boulevard de Clichy.
1910		In the spring, Picasso begins painting works in which the forms are broken up into small planes, making them more and more difficult to read.
	Summer	At Cadaqués
1911	Summer	Trip to Céret (where Braque joins him).
	October	The Cubist room at the Salon d'Automne scandalizes the public (Picasso and Braque do not exhibit). Beginning of Picasso's relationship with Eva Gouel; she will be evoked in his paintings by the words "Ma jolie".
1912	Summer	Trip to Céret and then to Sorgues, near Avignon (where Braque joins him).
	October	Picasso moves to a new studio at 242, boulevard Raspail.
1913	March	Trip to Céret. Evolution of Cubism towards very flat compositions made up of large planes, and the reappearance of color.
	Late Sept.	Picasso moves to a new studio at 5 bis, rue Schœlcher.
1914	August 2	Declaration of war. Braque and Derain are mobilized.
	November	Picasso returns to Paris after spending the summer in Avignon.
1915	December	Picasso meets Jean Cocteau.
	Dec. 14	Eva dies of tuberculosis.
1916	October	Picasso moves to Montrouge.
1917	February	Departure for Rome with Jean Cocteau to work on the sets and costumes for Diaghilev's ballet "Parade". It was on this occasion that he met Olga Khokhlova, one of the dancers in the troupe.
	November	Picasso returns to Paris with Olga and lives in Montrouge.

Head of a Woman (Fernande)

Autumn 1909,
Paris

This head came after a long series of portraits of Fernande made at Horta in the summer of 1909, in which he decomposed the features of his companion into small facets. It is surprising to note that in this case, a sculpture, he made use of a technique that takes on its full meaning when applied to two-dimensional representations (where forms must be fragmented in order to be shown flat). The head may still present the monolithic aspect of traditional sculpture, but the way in which it was modelled, with a series of rounded or hollow volumes (sometimes arbitrarily placed: a hollow being put where normally there should be a bump), creates breaks in what could be called the "epidermis" - to use Kahnweiler's term - of the sculpture, and these serve to catch the light. The importance of this work lies in the fact that it introduced discontinuity into the representation of volume, thus opening the way for experimentation with open forms and transparency in 20th-century sculpture.

Man with a Mandolin
Oil on canvas
162 x 71 cm

Man with a Mandolin

Autumn 1911,
Paris

Man with a Guitar

Autumn 1911 - [1913],
Paris

The main problem was still: how to represent, as objectively as possible, a three-dimensional figure on a two-dimensional surface without resorting to illusionistic devices? As Cubism progressed in its search, it came up with new solutions: in the *Man with a Mandolin,* the figure, which is indistinguishable from the background, has

Head of a Woman (Fernande)
Bronze
40.5 x 23 x 26 cm

Man with a Guitar
Oil on canvas
154 x 77.5 cm

are further references to reality. The two paintings are both practically monochromatic (representing objects in color brings the painter's subjectivity into play). A surprising feature to note is their apparently unfinished aspect. This was a common practice for Picasso (as it had been for Cézanne before him), and one that was particularly well-suited to Cubist representation: a certain number of clues having been given to the spectator, it was up to him to complete the picture mentally (since he was obliged to re-compose it anyway). Both paintings were enlarged by the addition of an extra strip of canvas at the bottom.

Still Life with Chair Caning

Spring 1912,
Paris

This painting was a revolution all to itself: for the artist used not only his traditional tools (brushes and paint), but he also introduced a real object into the picture, thus circumventing the need to represent it: an actual piece of oilcloth imitating chair caning, affixed to the canvas, does the duty of representing a chair. Paradoxically - and ironically - enough, the piece of oilcloth is itself an imitation, and this gives a humorous twist, a touch of kitsch to the picture. Apart from this element of collage - a major innovation, though no one could predict, at this date, what the future of this new technique would be -, the painting presents all of the main characteristics of the Cubist works of 1912: the pictorial space is flat, its

been broken up into little facets; the homogeneity of the form has been completely destroyed, flattened out, with the result that the picture becomes extremely difficult to read (this is one of the characteristic traits of what is known as the Analytic, or Hermetic, phase of Cubism, during the years 1910-1911). It was no doubt to avoid this pitfall that Picasso reworked his Man with a Guitar: in order to better define the figure, he repainted around it a monochrome area which covers some of the small fragmented planes (still partially visible underneath), and he kept certain visual clues to permit the identification of the forms: hair, eyes, nose, moustache, and pipe for the head of the guitarist; the guitar, with its fretted neck and sound-hole, the music score, a glass on the table, the carved feet of the chair, and the enigmatic letters KOU,

Still Life with Chair Caning
Oil and oilcloth on canvas, rope
29 x 37 cm

two-dimensionality being accentuated by the flatness of the piece of oilcloth, and objects in space are represented as if seen from several different sides (and not from a single point of view, as in traditional linear perspective). This necessarily entails the fragmentation of the objects, since several different aspects must be shown (in other words, what is represented is what is *known* about the objects, rather than what is seen from one given angle: the pipe stem is in perspective, while the bowl is represented as a white circle, as if seen from above), yet these objects remain recognizable just the same: pipe, newspaper (denoted by the first three letters of the French word "journal"), stemmed glass, lemon slice, knife, scallop shell, these all seem to have been placed on the caned chair or on a table that apparently coincides with the oval of the canvas itself. As a final whimsical touch, Picasso used a real piece of rope to frame the picture, an allusion to the ornamental trim used on tablecloths to highlight the shape of the table. The colors are in the characteristic grey and ocher monochrome, except for the naturalistic yellow of the lemon slice. Part of the right-hand side of the painting has been deliberately left unfinished; the unsized canvas is visible.

placed the use of paint. Pencil marks visible at the edges of the cuts show that there was sometimes a preliminary drawing, an outline into which the pieces of paper were fitted. In other cases, the paper was used directly in the freer technique of the assemblage: the paper being re-cut and moved around - which is probably why it was only pinned - until the right form and position had been found. This was the case especially where cut-out paper was used in conjunction with drawing. The paper was either cut into a shape that served to represent an object (like the bottle and guitar body in *Guitar, Glass, and Bottle of Vieux Marc)*, or, given an apparently random shape, it was then integrated into the play of lines composing the painting's spatial organization.

What role does the *papier collé* play? Sometimes it is presented just as what it is: a piece of sheet music *(Violin and Sheet Music)*, a pack of cigarettes *(Glass, Ace of Clubs, Pack of Cigarettes);* or it can be part of a whole which it represents, like printed wallpaper, or newspaper. And at other times, it was used simply as a colored surface (thus giving Picasso the means to reintroduce color, as in *Landscape at Céret)*. In any event, the *papier collé* served to introduce several levels of reality into the repre-

The papiers collés

1912-1914

Picasso and Braque, who had been pursuing their work in such extraordinarily close collaboration since 1908, were both concerned with the problem of keeping the content of their paintings related to the world of real objects, for the Cubist mode of representation threatened to render these undecipherable. This is why they began to introduce into their paintings certain visual clues, such as letters, imitation wood textures, and, starting in the autumn of 1912, elements made of paper.

The technique of *papier collé* (pasted paper) consists in the use of a sheet of paper as a support, onto which are pasted - or sometimes only pinned - various kinds of paper, newspaper, colored paper, wallpaper (flowered, or imitating wood, marble, etc.). Certain work, such as *Violin or Violin and Sheet Music,* were made entirely out of pieces of paper cut out and then assembled into the form of an object; paper thus re-

Violin and Sheet Music
Paris, Autumn 1912
78 x 63.5 cm

Glass, Ace of Clubs, Pack of Cigarettes
Paris,
Spring 1914
Papiers collés, oil, pastel and graphite
49 x 64 cm

sentation, and at times with a high degree of sophistication: in *Glass, Ace of Clubs, Pack of Cigarettes*, the pack of cigarettes is real: the playing card is a drawn imitation that has been cut out and glued: the piece of paper that serves as a background to the still life is an imitation of wood grain onto which the artist has painted, in *trompe-l'oeil* fashion, an ornamental molding. The space of the composition is modified by the addition of this paper, which, being flat itself, accentuates the two-dimensionality of the canvas. But in other instances it can introduce an element of relief, and in particular when it has been pinned: In the *Bottle of Wine and Die*, there is a feeling of volume to the die because it has been pinned to the paper, and so casts a real shadow.

Constructions and relief-paintings

1912-1914

The year 1912 saw the appearance of Picasso's first three-dimensional works made by assemblage, at a time when he was looking for other than purely pictorial means of representing objects and using collage techniques to this end. The two little guitars of 1912 are, in a sense, the projection into three dimensions of an object that he had often represented in his canvases, using principles that he had applied in his painting and that were just as foreign to tradi-

tional sculpture; they are open sculptures, the form is discontinuous (the neck and body of the guitar do not have a continuous contour). And the materials used are more those of the do-it-yourselfer than those of the sculptor: cardboard, paper, string, glue.

In 1914, Picasso began making objects that partook of both painting and sculpture - painted sculpture or painting in relief - which can be called constructions (when they are fully three-dimensional) or relief-paintings (those that are meant to hang on a wall like a painting), and which introduced a new experience of space and light. The most unexpected, yet often the most commonplace, materials were used for the construction of these small pieces, thus adding to their charm, just as the great care that went into making them grants them the aura of precious objects. Taking an empty tin box of powdered milk - from the "Compagnie française du lait sec", according to the label, which still exists -, Picasso cut, bent, and painted it, transforming it into a still life: *Bottle of Bass, Glass and Newspaper*. Using another piece of tin, cut and painted (the paint following the formal clues given by the cut-out shapes), and set against a background in a frame, he created a veritable painting in relief: *Glass, Newspaper, and Die*. Three wooden boxes were pressed into service to present small still lifes made of pieces of wood or cut and painted tin (the covers of these boxes were used as panels for small paintings). In such

Room 4

Guitar
Paris, December 1912
Cardboard, paper, string, oil, pencil
33 x 18 x 9.5 cm

Bottle of Bass, Glass, and Newspaper
Paris, Spring 1914
Cut and painted tin, sand, paper
20.7 x 14 x 8.5 cm

works, Picasso could give free rein to his love for discarded objects, taking them out of their utilitarian context and transforming them for his own artistic purposes.

Guitar

[Spring 1913],
[Céret]

If it weren't for a *papier collé* which is almost identical to this painting, and which contains the clues necessary for its identification (a small, pinned paper disk serves to represent the guitar's sound hole), there would be no reason to consider this virtually abstract composition as the representation of a guitar. And if one does not look closely enough, one might even think that it is a paper collage. In fact, it is an oil painting on canvas made with the help of stencils. The painter used a very simple and low-key color-scheme, harmonized with the color of the canvas itself, which has been left unpainted in two places.

Guitar
Oil on canvas
87 x 47.5 cm

Mandolin and Clarinet
Painted wood and pencil
58 x 36 x 23 cm

Man with a Pipe

[Spring 1914],
[Paris]

The collage technique, inaugurated in the *Still Life with Chair Caning* in 1912, was again used here: the smoker's shirtfront is in fact a large piece of red and white upholstery material with small flower designs. From the shape of the piece of material (which is visible through the layers of overpainting), it would seem that it served, at first, to represent the back of an armchair whose carved wooden feet are visible at the bottom of the painting. The figure of the man has become indistinguishable from the chair. His presence is indicated by a few minimal signs: one hand holding a white pipe, the other a newspaper. Behind can be seen a section of ornamental molding. The large

Mandolin and Clarinet

[Autumn 1913],
Paris

The experiment with the treatment of volume by means of facets in the *Head of a Woman* of 1909, and the introduction of open and discontinuous forms in his paintings starting in the summer of 1910, enabled Picasso to make the decisive break with traditional sculpture: from now on, forms that were full would be turned inside out, volumes decomposed into sets of planes, creating a complex interplay between full and empty space, the concave and the convex, frontal and lateral views. Here, the body of the mandolin has been represented by its absence, an empty space defined by the oval section cut out of a piece of wood, and the sound-hole, which should be a hollow space, is a round piece standing out in relief on the neck. The neck and body of the guitar, which should be in the same plane, are perpendicular. Except for the machine-made cylinder used for the clarinet, all of the other wooden parts of this construction came from pieces of scrap, a material that Picasso was particularly fond of working with.

Man with a Pipe
Oil and textile on canvas
138 x 66.5 cm

The Absinth Glass
Painted bronze,
sand and absinth spoon
21.5 x 16.5 x 8.5 cm

superimposed geometric planes, which are characteristic of what is called Synthetic Cubism, make for a very flat representation which would be completely abstract were it not for these figural indications.

The Absinth Glass

Spring 1914, Paris
Gift of Michel and Louise Leiris, 1984
On loan from the Musée National d'Art Moderne

Using unusual materials and unorthodox methods, Picasso made constructions and reliefs out of wood, cardboard and sheet metal to work on three-dimensional representation. In the Spring of 1914 appeared this bronze *Absinth Glass,* cast after a wax original. The return to traditional forms here is only superficial, however. The six versions are one-of-a-kind pieces, for Picasso decorated each of these first painted bronzes differently: some are brightly colored, with a red stem and a red and blue spotted cup, while others, like this one, are austere, sandy-colored and painted white on the bottom. These are variations on the well-known theme of the glass, one of the favorite motifs of Cubist iconography. While the mode of representation - an open form which is particularly appropriate for rendering the transparency of glass - belongs to the established conventions of Cubism, there is a surprise effect in the pre-

sence of a real object. The openwork spoon (which would channel, if it were not made of bronze also, the sugar dissolved by the absinth poured over it), is a familiar object of the times which strikes us by its old-fashioned charm today.

Glass, Pipe, Ace of Clubs and Die

Summer 1914,
Avignon

Here, more than in any of the other constructions of the year 1914, Picasso succeeded perfectly in making a painting in relief: the round format, reminiscent of the "tondos" of the Italian Renaissance, gives it a very noble appearance and raises it to the level of "high art"; and yet a very commonplace object, a box cover or mirror frame, was used as a support for the composition. The elements in relief define the objects of the still life: the piece of molding indicates the edge of the table (it is also represented by the round shape of the support) which holds a glass - half carved into the wood -, a die (which, ironically enough for a Cubist work, is cylindrical and not cubic), a pipe whose bowl is in high relief, and a playing card made from a piece of sheet-metal. All the while working in relief, Picasso continued to practise one of the principles of Cu-

Glass, Pipe, Ace of Clubs, and Die
Painted wood and metal
ø 34 cm x 8.5 cm

bism: the representation of multiple aspects of an object (which is shown as if seen from several different sides simultaneously, to give as complete an image as possible). Half of the glass was painted - with rounded forms - on the piece of wood that represents it, the other half as an angular form on the surface of the painting, and nearby as an outline; the playing card in relief was represented twice, by means of a slight rotation of the form; as for the table, it was evoked both by the plane surface of the support, made to look like fake green marble, and by the section of molding. In this way, what is painted re-presents what is in volume.

The Painter and His Model

Summer 1914,
Avignon

In the midst of his cubist activity, while he was producing works such as the one described above, Picasso painted this picture, which is all the more surprising for being the only one of its kind from this date. Being largely unfinished (to what extent was this deliberate?), this work is as much a drawing as it is a painting. An inveterate improviser, Picasso took what was closest at hand: a kitchen towel with a fine weave (its red stripe is still visible at the bottom), which he prepared with a white ground, and onto which he drew very precisely the elements of his composition: in a studio interior (as indicated by the easel and a palette on the wall), a seated painter contemplates his model as she unveils herself. Although the figuration is traditional and naturalistic (with, as always, certain expressive distortions such as the artist's large hand on his thigh, and the model's curious anatomy), the pictorial space shows the effects of Cubism: it has no depth (the background seems to coincide with the surface of the canvas), in spite of certain traditional perspective cues (the foreshortening of the chair legs). This mysterious painting, which features for the first time one of Picasso's fundamental themes - the painter and his model -, was discovered only after the artist's death, having been kept secret because the model was most probably Eva Gouel, his beloved "ma jolie", who died in 1915.

The Painter and His Model
Oil and pencil on canvas
58 x 55.9 cm

Violin
Cut, folded, and painted sheet metal
100 x 63.7 x 18 cm

that time and that would be abstract were it not for certain elements of reference - "f" holes, strings, bridge - to keep it on this side of representational art.

Man before a Fireplace

1916,
Paris

Cubism has become a style; we are now far from the sensitive analysis of forms that led to the refined paintings of 1912. A series of large geometric planes characteristic of what is known as Synthetic cubism serve to define an unengaging, rigid figure, which is relieved by the decorative application of little dots on some of its surfaces. This abstract representation interpenetrates with that of the chimney, which is easily recognizable with its mantelpiece, posts, blower (even the shell-shaped handle is visible), and a large mirror in a baroque frame sur-

Violin

[1915],
Paris

The violin may be recognized by the "f" holes, which, normally, are scroll-shapes cut into the sound-box on either side of the strings, but which have been given here a rectangular shape that is both hollow and in relief. One of the characteristic traits of Cubist sculpture is this non-imitational way of representing objects, by means of a transposition of forms: the hollow pans and those in relief, or the negative and positive spaces, no longer correspond to the original volumes: at the top of the violin, a folded element in relief stands for the strings, which are also represented below by a wide longitudinal space between the "f" holes, like a hollow at the heart of the instrument. Picasso made this violin out of a single sheet of metal, which he cut and folded (in such a skilful way that one has to examine the contours and folds very closely in order to reconstitute the original surface), and then painted (he was strongly drawn to the idea of painting sculpture), to create a form made up of large geometric planes, just like those that can be seen in his paintings of

Man before a Fireplace
Oil on canvas
130 x 81 cm

Portrait of Olga in an Armchair
Oil on canvas
130 x 88.8 cm

mounting it, all of which exists in a twisted, Cubist space suggested by a number of formulas (the mantelpiece whose top is parallel to the picture plane, the impossible perspective of the fireplace) that give this painting a somewhat stereotyped aspect.

Portrait of Olga in an Armchair

Autumn 1917,
Montrouge

This apparently classical portrait represents Olga Khokhlova, a member of the Ballets Russes company whom Picasso met in Rome in February 1917 and married the following year. The drawing is indeed quite classical, and reminiscent even of the manner of Ingres by its sinuous line and minutely rendered details: note the transparency of the material of the dress, the floral designs of the armchair cover, the colored patterns of the fan. Yet this image of the beautiful, distinguished, and cosmopolitan Olga is completely idealized as compared to the photograph which probably inspired it. At the same time, the painting looks like a collage, as if the form created by the female figure and the material of the armchair had been cut out and stuck on the background. In spite of the illusionistic rendering of her body (modelling of the neck and arms), the overall effect is one of flatness. Olga and the armchair seem to be floating in a nonexistent space, and independently of the fact that the painting is unfinished.

Room 5

The *Donation Picasso*
Picasso's Personal Collection

Picasso had often expressed the wish that part of his personal collection - that is, the works of artists other than himself that were in his possession - be given to the French nation and made public, with a dedication by him "To young painters". Respecting his wishes, Paulo and Jacqueline Picasso (with the consent of his other heirs) generously donated about fifty works which, after having been presented at the Louvre, found their place naturally, along with other works from the two dations, in the Hôtel Salé, among the Picassos whose company they shared for so many years. Picasso was very attached to his collection; in photographs of his various studios, these works can be made out in the midst of the general disorder, hanging on a wall, placed on the floor or on an easel, and sometimes even tucked away in the stacks of Picasso's own works, a testimony of the constant and intimate contact he maintained with those of Cézanne, Matisse, or the Douanier Rousseau, as if they were so many close friends. A strange collection it was, too, assembled by one who lacked the usual obsession of collectors for systematic and single-minded accumulations (in fact, he kept everything!). Rather, these works came together through chance meetings and finds, and exchanges made with painter friends. This collection reflects not the eye of a connoisseur, but the feelings of a painter who loved painting for its own sake. Who were his favorite painters? First of all, those who paved the way for 20th century painting: Cézanne especially, then Renoir, Degas, Vuillard, Gauguin; Henri Rousseau, the "naive" painter whom the future inventors of Cubism had adopted enthusiastically as one of the members of their avant-garde movement. And contemporary painters too: Matisse, his great rival, and Braque, Derain, Modigliani, Van Dongen, as well as younger painters like Balthus and Mirture inventors of Cubism had adopted enthusiastically as one of the members of their avant-garde movement. And contemporary paintThe works chosen for display at this particular point in the tour of the museum's collections were by artists who had a marked influence on Picasso's work of the first twenty years of this century (even if he did acquire some of them at a later date). The others are on display on the second floor, when this space is not occupied by temporary exhibitions.

In the studio of the rue des Grands-Augustins
Paris, 1942
(Archives Picasso, photo: H. Cartier-Bresson)

Degas

Paris,
1834-1917

Eleven monotypes (and a twelfth from the
1979 dation) which represent the strange
world of the "maisons closes" (bordellos):
the women are naked or clad only in black
stockings, waiting for clients, resting between "tricks", or celebrating with the
Madam. Provocative by their subject as well
as by their style, these prints, some of which
were used to illustrate Maupassant's *La
Maison Tellier*, must have appealed to Picasso especially, for eroticism was an ever-
present element in his work, either in a hidden form or brazenly explicit, from the
Demoiselles d'Avignon (which is a bordello
scene) to the engravings of the spring of
1970, which feature Degas himself as a witness to indescribable orgies. As an engraver,
Picasso must have been charmed by the monotype technique, in which a single impression is made from a drawing executed with
thick ink.

Degas: In the Salon
[1879]
Monotype
16.4 x 21.5 cm

Cézanne: View of Château-Noir
1905
Oil on canvas
74 x 94 cm

Cézanne

Aix-en-Provence,
1839-1906

"Do I know Cézanne! Why he was my one and only master", Picasso told Brassaï in 1943. We have already mentioned the decisive influence that the painter from Aix had on the elaboration of Cubism. He is represented in the collection by three major paintings and a watercolor: *The Bathers*, ac-

Renoir: Bather Seated in a Landscape,
also known as Eurydice
[1895-1900]
Oil on canvas, 116 x 89 cm

quired in 1957, whose theme underlies the creation of *Les Demoiselles d'Avignon*; *The Sea at l'Estaque*, acquired most likely after the war, and a surprising *View of Château-Noir* (the name of Cézanne's estate near Aix-en-Provence where he went to paint his subjects outdoors), which has a matte appearance ("Cézanne forbade Vollard to varnish his paintings", Jacqueline Picasso pointed out to André Malraux), and which was probably the first Cézanne that Picasso bought from the art dealer Ambroise Vollard, sometime before 1936. Picasso's bond with Cézanne continued even after death, one could say, for he was buried at Vauvenargues at the foot of the most famous of the Cézannian sites, the Montagne Sainte-Victoire.

Renoir

Limoges 1841 - Cagnes-sur-Mer 1919

Renoir is represented by seven works of very different kinds: nudes, portraits, a landscape, a still life, and the project for a mythological decoration. The most impressive of the works here is the *Large Bather Seated in a Landscape*, whose generous and monumental anatomy invariably brings to mind the colossal female figures painted by Picasso in the early Twenties. Visible here, in details like the two young girls in the background adorning a statue with garlands, and the bather's name, Eurydice, is the same antique inspiration as in works by Picasso such as *The Source and Three Women at the Spring*.

Henri Rousseau: Portrait of a Woman
[1895]
Oil on canvas
160 x 105 cm

Henri Rousseau

Laval 1844 - Paris 1910

"Picasso, you and I are the two greatest artists of our time, you in the Egyptian style, and I in the modern style." In these words, the Douanier Rousseau (a *"douanier"* is a customs official) acknowledged Picasso's talent, and by the same token his own. As for Picasso, he had a great admiration for this "naïve" painter, whose sincerity and genuineness appealed to and encouraged him at a time when he was striving to renew the language of painting. It was while browsing in the shop of the "père" Soulié, in 1908, that Picasso found the large *Portrait of a Woman,* whose head he had noticed sticking out of a dusty pile of paintings; the antique dealer asked him 5 francs for it, pointing out that the canvas was still good and could be used again! Not long after, from Vollard this time, Picasso acquired another painting by Rousseau, a sort of large historical composition that was probably inspired by a photograph, entitled: *The Representatives of Foreign Powers Coming to Salute the Republic as a Gesture of*

Peace (the symbol of the French republic, Marianne, dressed in red, holds a crown above the head of President Armand Fallières). This work provoked general hilarity when it was shown at the Salon des Indépendants in 1907. Particularly close to Picasso's heart were the little self-portrait and portrait of Rousseau's second wife which he bought from Paul Rosenberg at some time after 1938.

Matisse

Le Cateau-Cambresis 1869 - Nice 1954

Picasso's lifelong friendship with Matisse (they first met in 1906) was characterized by an odd mixture of respect, esteem, rivalry, and reserve, each one considering the other as his equal, and thus as a competitor, even though their respective paths were radically different; as opposed as "the North Pole and the South Pole", as Picasso is said to have put it. There were seven paintings by Matisse in his collection. A portrait of Matisse's daughter, *Marguerite,* painted in 1907, which he obtained in exchange for one of his still lifes in that same year, presents an extreme simplification of the drawing and colors that do not render volume. It must have been of great interest to the

Matisse: Still Life with Oranges
1912
Oil on canvas
94 x 83 cm

Derain: Portrait of a Young Girl
1914
Oil on canvas
61 x 50 cm

and not the donation) are from 1908, but are similar to the large composition of the preceding year. The *Portrait of a Young Girl*, a rigorous and austere work, probably dates from 1914. In that year, Picasso, Braque, and Derain all spent the summer at Avignon, a vacation that was brutally interrupted by the declaration of war, which occasioned a memorable separation at the train station, as his two friends left to serve under the flag.

Braque

Argenteuil 1882 - Paris 1963

The bond of friendship between Braque and Picasso, their intimately related trajectories, and especially their close association during the years from 1907 until the war, are well-known facts. As Braque later reminisced, "We lived in Montmartre, saw each other every day, talked together... during those years, Picasso and I spoke of things that no one will ever speak of again... It was a little like being roped together for mountain climbing." The *Still Life with a Bottle* from 1910-1911, "a painting that could be signed Picasso, a fraternal painting", wrote Malraux, was a gift or an exchange between the two artists, and shows

painter of the *Demoiselles d'Avignon* who was himself simplifying forms along the lines of Iberian art. Then there is the masterful *Still Life with Oranges*, undeniably the outstanding masterpiece of the collection, painted in Tangiers in 1912 and bought by Picasso in 1944. Of the two alpine landscapes from 1901, Picasso once said: "It takes a painter to see that here, already, is all the essence of Matisse! "The *Bouquet of Flowers in a Chocolate Pot* of 1902 was with Picasso when he left for Royan in 1939, at the beginning of the hostilities. The *Seated Young Girl* of 1942 and the *Tulips and Oysters on a Black Ground* of 1943 were both part of an exchange between the two painters.

Derain

Châtou 1880 - Garches 1954

Picasso and Derain met in 1906. Their interest in Cézanne and his influence on their work was a common ground between them, as was their affinity for primitive art. Derain's *Grandes Baigneuses*, exhibited at the salon des Indépendants of 1907, did not go unnoticed by Picasso, who was working on the *Demoiselles d'Avignon* at the time. *The Bathers* here (part of the 1979 dation,

Braque: Still Life with a Bottle
1910-1911
Oil on canvas
55 x 46 cm

Braque: The Guitar. Statue d'épouvante
Late 1913
Pasted paper, charcoal and gouache on paper
73 x 100 cm
1990 Dation

the closeness of their work. *The Guitar* from 1913 illustrates the technique of *papiers collés* - "a paperistic and dustful process" - which Braque invented in the autumn of 1912, and which Picasso also adopted. Cut-out and pasted pieces of wallpaper of uni-form color or imitating wood, touched up with charcoal, were used to represent a still life on an oval table: a guitar, a glass, sheet music, and a real movie program from Sorgues (near Avignon) announcing a film whose title, *Statue of Horror,* adds to the complexity of the different levels of reality presented in this *papier collé* that has a foretaste of Surrealism.

Miró

Barcelona 1893-1984

As soon as he arrived in Paris in 1919, Mirels of reality presented in this rgues (near Avignon) announ *Self-Portrait,* which he gave to Picasso in 1921, shows an obvious debt to Cubism in its style. The *Portrait of a Spanish Dancer* was a later acquisition. The two painters were dosely associated during the years of the Surrealist movement.

Miró: Self-Portrait
1919
Oil on canvas
73 x 60 cm

Room 5

Room **6**   The Classical Period

1918-1924

1918	July 12	Wedding of Picasso and Olga at the Russian church, rue Daru, Paris.
	Summer	Biarritz, guest of Mrs. Errazuriz.
	Nov. 8	Picasso meets André Breton.
	Nov. 9	Death of Apollinaire.
	Late Dec.	Picasso and Olga move to 23, rue La Boétie.
1919	Dec. 3	Death of Renoir.
1920		Beginning of what is known as his Classical period, inspired by the art of Antiquity and Ingres.
1921	Feb. 4	Birth of Picasso and Olga's son Paulo.
	Summer	At Fontainebleau. Throughout these years Picasso worked on theater decors and costumes, especially for the Ballets Russes.

Olga, Picasso and Cocteau
in 1917
(Archives Picasso)

The Happy Family after Le Nain

Autumn 1917,
[Paris]

Picasso's interest in the painting of the Le Nain brothers is attested by the presence of two pictures in his personal collection: one of them is attributed to Louis Le Nain, and the other to one of his followers: the Master of the Procession of the Ram. The subject of the present work came from Louis Le Nain's The Happy Family (officially acquired by the Louvre in 1939), which he interpreted according to the aesthetic idiom that he was then practising: realism in the drawing, use of quite vivid colors applied with the small brushstrokes characteristic of his Cubist works at the time. The result is a transposition of the 17th-century painting: with respect to the forms (which dissolve into color), the definition of space (unrelated to conventional linear perspective, which, besides, was not always the Le Nains'forte: the figures here, out of proportion, float in a space without depth).

Bathers

Summer 1918,
Biarritz

For the first time since his childhood, Picasso was able to spend the summer by the sea. With his new bride, Olga, he went to Biarritz, having been introduced into high society by his collaboration with the Ballets Russes and his success as an artist. The pleasures of life on the beach and in the open air nourished his inspiration; this curious painting features - in a "post-card" setting complete with a sailboat, a lighthouse, and small white clouds - three bathers dressed in the swimming attire then in fashion for women at seaside resorts. Their oddly proportioned bodies are twisted and elongated into unusual attitudes (that are Picasso's interpretation of those in Ingres's Turkish Bath, but with an even more exaggerated mannerism). The bather in the striped swimsuit has been represented simultaneously with front and back views, proof of the lasting effects of Cubism's effort to show things from all different angles. The

Bathers
Oil on canvas
27 x 22 cm

The Happy Family, after Le Nain
Oil on canvas
162 x 118 cm

The Lovers
Oil on canvas
185 x 140 cm

scene takes place in a dreamlike decor in which the grey sand is strewn with strange, meticulously rendered stones. However rigorous the line may be, it does not serve the purposes of any realistic representation, and the bright colors make for a somewhat naive effect (reminiscent of the Douanier Rousseau), while at the same time the painting is full of cultural allusions; Greek vase painting, antique statuary, Botticelli, El Greco, Ingres, Seurat…

The Lovers

1919,
Paris

There is a famous painting by Manet called *Nana*, which shows a woman in petticoats standing before a mirror, doing her make-up, while a man dressed in evening clothes, complete with a top hat, sitting on a sofa, watches her. In this homage to Manet, and as usual when he based himself on the work of a past master, Picasso used the same elements but changed the scene so that now the man, who is easily recognizable with his moustache and black tuxedo, is shown embracing the woman, a courtesan, clad in a blue corset (she is probably sitting on his lap). The bouquet she is holding and the little cat drawn in charcoal on the white cover are allusions to another painting by Manet, *Olympia*. On the wall hang drawings that recall the Japanese prints that had had such a great influence on the Impressionist painters. In a large, childlike hand Picasso signed: Manet. At the same time, he introduced Cubist imagery (the newspaper *L'Intransigeant* on the floor, the glass in the man's hand, the molding of the wainscot), and as further evidence that the style of the painting descends in a large

Seated Woman
Oil on canvas
92 x 65 cm

the attitudes of the hands (one of which holds an elbow, while on the other she nonchalantly rests her head), which recalls those of the figures of Ingres.

Reading the Letter

1921,
[Paris]

The meaning of this painting, whose existence became known only after Picasso's death, is still a complete mystery: who are these two young men - related by their massive stature to the peplos-clad giantesses -, seated like antique gods in modern dress in a timeless, inhospitable landscape, rocky desert or seashore, set off by the magic glow of a bluish halo, entirely absorbed in the reading of a letter? Some have interpreted it as an evocation of the friendship between Picasso and Braque, or again between Picasso and Apollinaire (the book

Reading the Letter
Oil on canvas
184 x 105 cm

measure from Cubism: the figures are flat, superimposed or interlocking shapes, with extremely simplified, often geometric outlines.

Seated Woman

1920,
Paris

Picasso's work from the years 1920-1923 is usually spoken of in terms of classicism, because the themes - nude or draped female figures with Greek profiles - are obvious references to the world of Antiquity (which the painter rediscovered during his trip to Rome in 1917). But Picasso's classicism is one that has been completely reinterpreted and deviated from its original principles: the moderation of classical art has given way to its opposite. The seated woman here is a giantess, her hands and feet are huge, deformed, and she seems to be petrified in her drapery. The impression of volume is heightened by the contrast of light and shadow, which completely fills out the forms of the figure. In spite of the statuesque ponderousness, there is a certain elegance to

Three Women at the Spring
Red chalk and oil on canvas
200 x 161 cm

could serve as an attribute of the poet, and the Kronshtadt hat is similar to the one he used to wear; unless it is Cézanne's hat…). The way in which the color was applied, particularly for the clothes, is equally surprising; Picasso first outlined the areas to be painted (probably with the help of stencils) before filling them in, just like in a paint-by-number set for children.

Three Women at the Spring

Summer 1921,
Fontainebleau

The summer of 1921, spent at Fontainebleau, saw the creation of two major works (or rather four, since there were two slightly different versions of each): one in the Cubist vein, the *Three Musicians*, and the other in the Classical spirit, *Three Women at the Spring*, which was executed in red chalk and oils, somewhat like a gigantic drawing (a number of studies for it are in the museum's collections). In spite of Picasso's transpositions, such as the exaggeratedly filled-out bodies, these three figures are distant relatives of the stout young women that compose the austere Panathenaic procession on the famous Parthenon frieze: Greek profile, twisted strands of hair sometimes coiled into a chignon, drapery with deep folds that evoke the fluting of columns. Picasso probably also had in mind the version of Antiquity presented by Poussin in a painting like the *Shepherds of Arcady*, for here too the figures are characterized by a grave stillness, and rigorously structured by a rhythm of horizontal and vertical lines, which is interrupted by the skilfully composed circular movement of the hands.

The Village Dance

[1922],
[Paris]

Picasso frequently used pastel (a crayon made of compacted powdered pigment) for his large drawings at the beginning of the Twenties. This medium enables the artist to work on textural effects - grainy when the pastel is left in a pulverized form, or smooth when it is rubbed - and color effects ranging from the opaque to the transparent. Here, the painter, who never hesitated to use materials in an unconventional manner, used both pastel and oil on a canvas with a large weave that is still visible through the color. The dancers are as rigid as statues, their features unmoving and expressionless, their bodies pressed in an embrace that keeps them apart rather than joining them together; they are the melancholy paraphrase of the couple in Renoir's *Dance in the Country* (Musée d'Orsay, Paris), in which a man in a blue vest is dancing closely with his smiling partner in a white dress and whispering sweet nothings in her ear.

The Village Dance
Pastel and oil on canvas
139.5 x 85.5 cm

The Pipes of Pan

Summer 1923,
Antibes

This strange work shows two young men, one of whom is playing a set of reed pan-pipes, in a seaside setting, by a featureless sea that is probably the Mediterranean, under the stark noon sun (there are no shadows, except for the one cast vertically by one of the legs of the musician). The sparsely furnished background is indicated by a few plain geometric blocks, disposed like so many illusionistic theater props on a stage, against a backdrop painted in two different blues to represent the sea and the sky. The figure playing the pipes of Pan recalls the shepherds of Antiquity, but his body is common and devoid of grace. The two young men seem to ignore one another, the musician being absorbed in his playing, while the other figure simply poses with a vacant stare, somewhat in the manner of the figures painted by Piero della Francesca. More immediate than the reference to Antiquity - with a distant allusion to the theme of Apollo and Marsyas - is the reference to Cézanne, whose bathers have the same massive bodies, and even the same ill-fitting swimsuits. Simplicity, grandeur, balance, it is terms such as these that come to mind to describe this unusual picture whose meaning remains obscure (for a figurative representation is not necessarily easier to read than a Cubist work), and which Picasso always kept in his studio.

Paulo as Harlequin

1924,
Paris

On February 4, 1921, Olga gave birth to a boy, Paulo; here was a new model to whom the painter could give all his attention and tenderness. In this portrait, we recognize the same dark eyes and steady gaze as his father's, and a Harlequin's costume like the ones that Picasso was so fond of (and in which he had already represented himself), expressions of the bond between father and son. This painting, which seems quite conventional with its detailed figuration (could it be that the bold inventor of Cubism had quieted down?), was deliberately left unfinished: the background was only lightly brushed in with paint (which defines

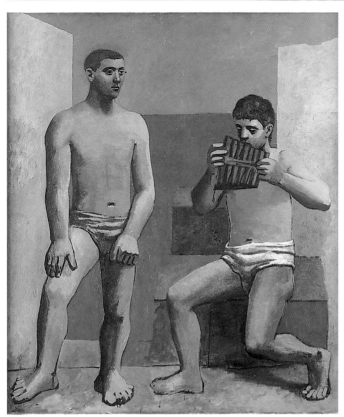

The Pipes of Pan
Oil on canvas
205 x 174 cm

no space), and the bottom of the chair and the child's feet (the artist even left a pentimento by the right leg) have not been painted at all. The child and chair seem to be floating on the surface of the canvas, completely unattached, being merely colored surfaces themselves (only the child's face and hands have been modelled to give the illusion of volume), which contributes to the impression of fragile beauty we get from this too-formal, somewhat sad, but serene little boy.

Paulo as Harlequin
Oil on canvas
130 x 97.5 cm

Room 6 *bis* Picasso and the Theater

The world of the stage, of the *café-concert,* and of the itinerant circus performers was a familiar one to Picasso and had been the source of some of his favorite subjects at the beginning of the century. It is not surprising, then, that he himself came to work for the theater, primarily between 1916 and 1924. At the origin of this new adventure was his encounter with Jean Cocteau in 1915. The young poet soon managed to enlist his collaboration to design the costumes and decors for a ballet project in which he, Cocteau, was writing the subject and Erik Satie the music. This ballet was to be called *Parade* and performed by the troupe directed by Serge Diaghilev, the Ballets Russes.

Sketch for the curtain of *Parade*
1917
Watercolor and graphite
27.3 x 39.5 cm

Parade

1916-1917

At first, the theme of the ballet was a circus parade, performed by an acrobat, a Chinese conjuror, and a little American girl who show samples of their routines to attract the public. But, as Picasso progressed in his work, he modified Cocteau's original scenario by introducing new characters: the so-called "managers", which were huge, inhuman figures, in fact living stage sets made from three-meter-high Cubist constructions actually worn by the dancers, who were completely hidden within. The museum owns many of the sketches for the various costumes, and particularly for the three managers: the "French manager" with his moustache, evening clothes and top hat, smoking a pipe and carrying a walking stick at the end of an extraordinarily long arm; the "American manager" with skyscrapers and flags on his back; and the third, a negro figure on horseback (for the actual performance, only the horse - a wood and cloth construction animated by two dancers hidden inside - was retained). The stage decor designed by Picasso featured a gypsy hut surrounded by skyscrapers and was executed in the Cubist style. The drop curtain was a gigantic affair, 10 meters high and 17 meters wide (it is preserved today at the Musée National d'Art Moderne in Paris), and represented itinerant performers, including Harlequin, Columbine, a winged girl on a winged horse, and musicians in a scene

Sketch of the stage curtain for *Le Tricorne*
London, 1919
Graphite and black pencil
28 x 26.5 cm

whose romanticism and serenity must have contrasted sharply with the aggressiveness and modernity of the ballet itself, which mixed painting and dance in such a new way. The opening performance was held at the Théâtre du Châtelet in Paris on May 18, 1917. It was greeted enthusiastically by some, while others, who considered any avant-garde expression as unpatriotic because the country was still at war (the word "Kubism" was coined), expressed their hostility by shouting *"Sales boches!"* ("Dirty Krauts!") when the final curtain came down.

Le Tricorne

1919

In collaboration with the dancer and choreographer Massine, Diaghilev produced a Spanish ballet with music by Manuel de Falla ("The Three-cornered Hat") and based on a story from a picaresque novel: an old provincial governor in the south of Spain in the 18th century falls in love with a miller's wife, whom he tries to seduce, but without success; he is finally overthrown by the villagers and the ballet ends with scenes of great rejoicing. Picasso agreed to design the decors and the costumes: the drop curtain represented the end of a corrida (with the dead bull being taken away) as seen through the arcade of the spectator's box above the arena. The decor featured the in-

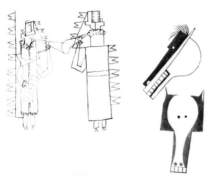

Sketch for a costume for *Parade*
1917
Watercolor and graphite
20.5 x 28 cm

terior of the miller's house, with a view, through an arch, of the landscape and village beyond; the costumes were traditional and very colorful. The first performance of this dazzling, if rather conventional, ballet was held in London (where Picasso spent three months working on its preparation) on July 22nd, 1919.

Pulcinella

1920

With the production of Pulcinella (the commedia dell'arte character known in English as Punch), Picasso found himself in the midst of the familiar world of his beloved Harlequin. Diaghilev and Massine chose Igor Stravinsky to compose music with themes derived from the 18th-century Neapolitan composer Pergolesi, on the following plot: Pulcinella, who is in love with Pimpinella, is beset by the amorous attentions of two young women who are themselves engaged and under the watchful eye of their respective fathers; after a series of misunderstandings, quarrels, and unexpected turns of events, all ends well, each marrying his chosen one. Picasso's collaboration with Diaghilev on this project took a rather stormy turn. The painter's sketches for the costumes called for modern dress (in the style of Offenbach) and his idea for the

decor involved a theater within the theater: on the stage was to be reproduced the boxes and ceiling of a Second Empire period theater, at the back of which there would be a second stage with a set representing a small street leading to a port with Mount Vesuvius in the background. When Picasso submitted his first sketches, Diaghilev rejected them outright and stormed out of the room. In the end, the set design was extremely simple, very Cubist: a small square framed by houses that look like playing cards, opening onto a view with a boat, the sea, and Mount Vesuvius under a full moon; the costumes were traditional: Pulcinella in a flowing white garment, sporting a pointed bonnet and a black mask with an enormous, grotesque nose. The first performance was held at the Paris Opera on May 15, 1920.

Cuadro Flamenco

1921

The theme of this show produced by Diaghilev was Spain, and it was performed by a Sevillan troupe of flamenco singers, dancers, and musicians at the Théâtre de la Gaité Lyrique in May 1921. Juan Gris was his first choice for the decors (Diaghilev wanted an artist who was as Spanish as his show), but because time was short, he deci-

Sketch for the costume of Pulcinella
Paris, 1920
Graphite and gouache
34 x 23.5 cm

Maquette for the stage curtain of Cuadro Flamenco
1921
Gouache, India ink, and graphite
23.5 x 34 cm

Room 6 *bis*

Maquette for the curtain of *Mercure*
[1924]
Pastel and black pencil
25 x 32 cm

ded on Picasso instead, settling for the first decor project for Pulcinella: on the stage, the representation of a theater with its boxes and spectators was used as a backdrop for the dances.

Mercure

1924

This ballet, a series of mythological episodes which featured, among others, the god Mercury (and, strangely enough, Punch), was choreographed by Léonide Massine (who had left the Ballets Russes) on a musical score by Erik Satie, and produced by Count Etienne de Beaumont. The drop curtain (today in the Musée National d'Art Moderne in Paris) had nothing to do with the theme of the ballet: the figures of Harlequin and Pierrot as musicians being composed of outlines and colored surfaces which did not coincide. Picasso created special stage sets called *"praticables"* that could be moved by the dancers during the performance. The costumes were of the tra-

Women Running on the Beach (The Race)
Dinard, Summer 1922
Oil on plywood
32.5 x 41.1 cm

Portrait of Erik Satie
Paris, May 19, 1920
Graphite and charcoal
62 x 47.7 cm

Portrait of Igor Stravinsky
Paris, May 24, 1920
Graphite and charcoal
61.5 x 48.2 cm

ditional kind for mythological subjects, except those for the three Graces, who were danced by men sporting black wigs and large red-painted breasts.

That same year, for Diaghilev's *Le Train Bleu,* a ballet set in a fashionable seaside resort, Picasso executed an enlarged version of his 1922 painting that represents two colossal, wild-haired *Women Running on the Beach,* dressed in classical drapery. The scenario was by Cocteau, the stage sets by Laurens, the costumes by Chanel, and the music by Darius Milhaud. Picasso made use of the same procedure in 1936 when he enlarged a gouache for the curtain of Romain Rolland's play, *Le 14 juillet.* Another product of the years he spent working for the theater is the series of masterful line drawings portraying such figures as Diaghilev, Satie, Stravinsky, Manuel de Falla, or Leon Bakst, who designed many decors and costumes for the Ballets Russes.

Portrait of S. Diaghilev and A. Seligsberg
[London], 1919
Graphite and charcoal
63.5 x 49.6 cm

Room 7   On the Fringes of Surrealism

1924-1929

1924	Summer	At Juan-les-Pins
	October	Publication of André Breton's *Manifeste du surréalisme*.
1925		All the while producing serene works in the Cubist vein, Picasso subjects the human figure to extreme and aggressive deformations.
1926	January	First issue of the *Cahiers d'art* edited by Christian Zervos.
1927		Picasso meets Marie-Thérèse Walter, with whom he will have a liaison until 1936.
	Summer	In Cannes.
1928	Summer	In Dinard.
1929		His relationship with Olga deteriorates more and more.

Marie-Thérèse Walter
in 1928
(Documentation du
musée Picasso)

Guitar
Cut, folded, and painted sheet metal
111 x 63.5 x 26.6 cm

The Kiss
Oil on canvas
130.5 x 97.7 cm

Guitar

1924,
Paris

The group of young people which formed around André Breton to create the Surrealist movement acknowledged their debt to the inventor of Cubism: Picasso's opposition to illusionistic representation had opened the way to a new approach to art. This is why a reproduction of this Cubist guitar was printed in the first issue of *La Révolution surréaliste* in December 1924. Breton wrote also that his first "encounter" with Picasso had been his discovery of the constructions of 1913 published in an issue of *Soirées de Paris*. Created some ten years later, this guitar was a natural descendant of these works. Made of a single sheet of metal that he cut, folded, and painted, it displays the characteristics of Cubist sculpture: an open form, discontinuity, and the play of full and empty spaces (the guitar's sound-hole is represented by a tin can that stands out - the only addition - and part of the neck is depicted by a hollow space); the colors, which play on the cut-out shapes, give rise to discrepancies in the definition of the contours, an effect that was constantly used in Cubist painting.

The Kiss

Summer 1925,
Juan-les-Pins

Those who had witnessed Picasso's return to figurative painting in 1917 and assumed that he had settled down in his career as an artist, just as he had in his private life (the church wedding and move to a chic area, far from his bohemian haunts), must have been completely bewildered to discover that the painter of the *Demoiselles d'Avignon* had lost none of his violence or need to transgress all taboos, be they artistic or moral. Before us is a couple in a passionate embrace, but it is quite impossible to make out just exactly what is going on, so closely entwined are the pieces of this puzzle: the man's left arm is visible, as he clasps his partner, whose head is thrown back, while her bare feet, which emerge from the lozenge-patterned dress, seem not to be touching the ground, and their two mouths are fused into one. This picture may lack explicitness (it has been titled variously *On the Beach* and *Seated Woman*), but there is no doubt as to Picasso's use of blatant sexual imagery: the man's nose and the woman's mouth evoke, respectively, male and female genitals. "Art is never chaste", Picasso used to say. A few years later, André Breton was to proclaim that "Beauty will be convulsive, if it is to be at all". What more appropriate terms to define this painting, in which the virulence of the colors and the ferocity of the deformations express so perfectly the frenzy of an embrace?

The Painter and His Model

1926,
[Paris]

In 1926 the art dealer Ambroise Vollard commissioned Picasso to engrave a series of plates to illustrate a novel by Balzac called *Le Chef-d'oeuvre inconnu* (the story of an old painter who is so obsessed with perfection that he ends up destroying his masterpiece by dint of working on it: through the tangle of lines and blotches of color, all that remains visible of his once-superb picture is a divinely painted woman's foot). The theme of the painter and his model - one of the fundamental themes of Western art - necessarily made its appearance in Picasso's work: here the composition is defined by a gigantic arabesque superimposed on a series of grey and white planes. The woman is shown lying down on the left, her arms crossed under a tiny head, and with a huge foot (probably an allusion to Balzac's story); the painter is on the right, separated from his model by the canvas on which he is working (part of it, tacked on the stretcher, is visible). The latter, holding his palette and seated on a chair, has been represented with his face in both frontal and profile views. Picasso violated the human figure, deforming the woman's body and displacing the features of the painter's face, yet without destroying it completely. The extreme right side of the picture has been left unfinished, showing that the composition

The Painter and His Model
Oil on canvas
172 x 256 cm

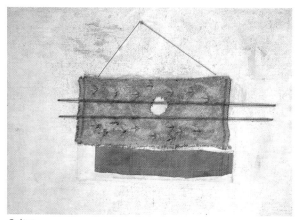

Guitar
String, newspaper, floor rag, nails on painted canvas
96 x 130 cm

was first drawn on the canvas (and reworked many times, judging by the numerous pencil strokes) before being painted (in fact, the background was filled in after the parts drawn in black paint). Although it may be fitting to speak of "writing" in connection with this picture, it had nothing to do with the "automatic writing" of the Surrealists.

of presenting so humble an artifact as a dirty floor rag aside, there is the disquieting fact of those long nails pointed at the spectator, and an uncommon aggressivity that charges the work with a magical, "intangible" quality: in fact, Picasso had even considered putting razor blades on the edges of the canvas to keep profanating hands at bay.

Guitar

Spring 1926,
Paris

Lautréamont, in his book *Les Chants de Maldoror* (1868), defined beauty as being like "the chance encounter of a sewing machine and an umbrella on a dissection table". Before the Surrealists ever appropriated this definition for their movement, and without being driven by the nihilistic and mocking spirit of the Dadaists, Picasso was sensitive to the beauty of commonplace objects and had felt the need to transgress the laws of painting in order to integrate them into a work of art. This is what he had done in his *Still Life with Chair Caning;* but here, with this guitar made out of a floor rag, a piece of newspaper, string, and nails, it was not so much a matter of integrating everyday objects into an artwork (which was the intention of the Cubist collages), as it was of exploiting the full range of their meanings: the provocative aspect

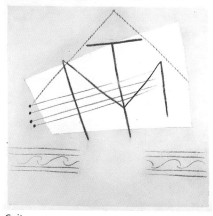

Guitar
Oil and charcoal on canvas
81 x 81 cm

Guitar

April 27, 1927,
Paris
1990 Dation

Who would have imagined it? In this work dated April 27, 1927 - the veiled confession of a secret love affair - we see a manifestation in Picasso's art of the young woman he loved: the painter reveals only the monogram - MT - of his new companion, Marie-Thérèse. Already in 1912, he had made the equally discreet revelation of the presence of a new woman in his life, Eva, by inscribing the words "Ma jolie" in his paintings. Here, the name is inscribed at the heart of the guitar, a metaphor for the female body and one of the principal iconographic motifs of Cubist still lifes: the painted quadrangular shape - which recalls the *papiers collés* - becomes a guitar thanks to such scanty graphic elements as the strings and the strap by which it hangs on the wall.

Painter with Palette and Easel
Oil on canvas
130 x 97 cm

Painter with Palette and Easel

1928

The painter this time is without the model who is represented in so many paintings and drawings by Picasso and is seated in an armchair with a curved back, a paintbrush and palette in his left hand, painting with his right hand on a blank canvas. His head seems to be composed of two interpenetrating profiles, one white and one black, with a pair of eyes placed at their intersection. The amoeba-like face is bordered by three straight strands of hair. With the help of Julio González, Picasso made three little painted sculptures (which differ only by their color) based on this particular head, assembled out of iron and steel (one of them is in the museum's collections).

scaffolding-like constructions surmounted by a little disk with three dots giving it the semblance of a human face. In the autumn, these little studies were given three-dimensional form in the Montparnasse studio of the sculptor Julio González, whom he had known since 1902. Thanks to his friend, he

Figure
Metal wire and sheet metal
60.5 x 15 x 34 cm

Figure

Autumn 1928,
Paris

During the summer of 1928, which he spent at Dinard, Picasso executed a series of drawings consisting of dots connected by lines,

was able to make up for what he lacked in tools, materials, and especially know-how, to enable him to realize a project that had been on his mind for several years: to make a monument to Guillaume Apollinaire, who had died in 1918. The idea of executing a monumental sculpture was what he was aiming at when he conceived these filiform constructions, veritable drawings in space (Picasso excelled in the transposition of one medium into another, making the most of their respective qualities), sculptures made of transparency and empty space. Several maquettes of these were produced; imposing, yet gracile constructions that display a masterful complexity in the spatial organization of their elements (the metal wire being bent, criss-crossed, and welded at "nodal" points). But when Picasso submitted these sculptures as models for a monument for the grave of Apollinaire in Père

Lachaise cemetery, they were turned down (the memorial to the poet that was ultimately placed in 1959 in the small park next to the church of Saint-Germain-des-Prés was the cast bronze *Head of a Woman*, a 1941 portrait of Dora Maar). A large-scale sculpture of this maquette was executed for the garden of the Picasso Museum in 1984.

Nude in an Armchair

1929,
Paris

Picasso was not a Surrealist painter. At no time did he belong to that movement, nor did he rely on the random and unconscious factors involved in Surrealist creation. But the Surrealists recognized him as one of their own, for his work referred not to

Nude in an Armchair
Oil on canvas
195 x 129 cm

conventional reality, but to the artist's "internal model" of it, to use Breton's words. This must have been some internal model! What has become of the women with graceful limbs, of the beautiful Olga? Or even of those antique goddesses with their placid beauty and statuesque immobility? Instead there is a shrieking woman, her head thrown back, with dishevelled hair and a gaping mouthful of teeth, limbs like tentacles around a horribly deformed body, displaying her unappetizing charms, flaccid breasts, anus, and gashed crotch, all this against an equally shrill background (strident colors of the mirror frame, armchair, and wallpaper). This excessiveness reveals the psychological and emotional charge that Picasso's painting had come to bear. It is not so much an expression of the woman's despair as that of the artist's own despairing of her: some have seen in this picture an anguished reflection of the bitter tensions in Picasso's relationship with his wife.

Seated Woman
Bronze
42.5 x 16.5 x 25 cm

Seated Woman

Spring 1929,
Paris

Fixed in bronze, this deformed, deliquescent blob, another product of Picasso's need to do violence to the human form, has nonetheless been left with enough anatomical features to be recognizable as a female figure: a long neck at the end of which is a small head; two breasts, one of which is pointing up and the other down, placed above a diminutive waist; the belly, pierced by a navel, and the buttocks (which should be out of sight, because the woman is seated) merge with the top of the right leg, at the end of which, like the other leg, there is a monstrous club-foot. The tentacle-like arms are wrapped pathetically around this misshapen body.

Second floor

Picasso as a Printmaker

One of the rooms on the second floor of the museum is used to present the collection of prints on a rotating basis, whenever the space is not occupied by a temporary exhibition.

Picasso's production as a printmaker was enormous, with over 2,000 prints catalogued in all, covering a wide range of techniques: notably, engraving, etching, drypoint, woodcut, monotype, lithography, linocut. Their number is actually greater because of the fact that he often turned out a series of different states of each print, reworking, improving, and modifying the drawing before reaching the final state. The prints for the 1979 dation were chosen from among the enormous body of work in Picasso's possession according to the following principle: since the Bibliothèque Nationale de France already owned a sizable collection of Picasso's prints (in their final state, for the copyright law requires that a copy of each published print be submitted to the Cabinet des Estampes), it seemed preferable for the museum to

The Frugal Repast
1904
Aquatint on zinc
46 x 37.8 cm

Still Life with Bunch of Keys
1912
Dry-point engraving on copper
21.8 x 27.9 cm

Face
1928
Lithography
20.6 x 14.2 cm

Sculptor and Model
Paris, March 21, 1933
Aquatint on copper
26.6 x 19.4 cm

assemble series of successive preliminary states, which are generally very rare and which enable us to follow, through modifications of details that are sometimes difficult to notice for the untrained eye, the progress of the artist's painstaking work (in some cases there is only one proof of a particular state, run off by the artist himself to get an idea of the plate's effect). Also selected - and a further rarity - were unpublished prints that had never officially been catalogued. The 1990 dation further completed this collection. When they were not printed by Picasso himself, the plates were handled by various printers: Eugène Delâtre, Louis Fort, Roger Lacourière, Aldo and Piero Crommelynck. The lithographs were printed by Mourlot, and the linocuts by Arnera at Vallauris.

Picasso never really learned the printmaker's craft (when he set out to make his first engraving, he did not realize that the printed plate would yield an inverted image, and that he would end up with a lefthanded figure!), but a lifelong practice taught him all the tricks of the trade (which, as usual, he enriched by introducing new, surprising, and often unorthodox techniques). It would be impossible to go into any detail about the museum's collection of around eighteen hundred prints, and so we will mention only the highlights of Picasso's production as a printmaker.

Ambroise Vollard, in 1913, published a series of fourteen etchings from 1904-1905 on the theme of the saltimbanques, which features the frail and slender figures of the Rose Period; this series includes the famous print called *The Frugal Repast*. In 1906-1907, at the same time that he was carving primitive-style wood sculptures, Picasso executed a number of woodcuts. Two books by the poet Max Jacob published by Kahnweiler, *Saint Matorel* in 1911 and *Le Siège de Jérusalem* in 1914, contain the most famous copper engravings from the Cubist period.

Second floor

The Weeping Woman
1937
Aquatint, dry-point engraving on copper,
with scraping
69.1 x 47.7 cm

David and Bathsheba (after Cranach), 2nd state
March 30, 1947
Pen and wash on zinc
65.7 x 50.2 cm

Afterwards, in the early Twenties, he executed a certain number of prints in conjunction with his painted work (and also began trying his hand at lithography), until 1924 when he engraved thirteen plates to illustrate Balzac's *Le Chef-d'oeuvre inconnu* (published by Vollard in 1931); it was in this series that he first began to treat what would become one of his favorite themes: the painter and his model. The year 1931 also saw the publication, by Albert Skira, of an edition of Ovid's *Metamorphoses*, illustrated by Picasso with thirty etchings depicting antique scenes with a very delicate line (the museum also owns the plates that were not used for this edition).

A series of one hundred plates engraved between 1930 and 1937 were assembled by Vollard for an edition named after him: the *Suite Vollard*. This series is noteworthy not only for its quality (Picasso worked a great deal on these plates, judging by the large number of preliminary states that exists for many of them), but also for its range of themes: the first twenty-seven prints are on a variety of subjects; the next five, grouped under the heading of "The Rape", depict the artist's erotic obsessions; these are followed by a series entitled "Rembrandt", after which come forty-six plates on the theme of "The Sculptor's Studio", which can be seen as portraying the twofold adventure that the artist was living at the time: there was a new woman in his life, Marie-Thérèse, and so a new model, whose beauty inspired Picasso to work at sculpture. The plates feature the same large heads as those sculpted at Boisgeloup in 1931, bearing witness to the continuous dialogue in Picasso's art between the different mediums that he used. The series continues with plates on the "Minotaur" and the "Blind Minotaur", in which the monstrous mythological creature who was half man and half bull is shown as a brutal lover, yet also as a fragile and even a mortal being, who may be seen as Picasso's emblem (this figure returns in the famous 1935 etching of *Minotauromachy*). Insofar as the *Suite Vollard* is concerned, no other museum has as rich a collection as the one here: the several extremely rare series of preliminary states included in these one hundred prints from the original dation were joined, in 1980, thanks to Madeleine Lacourière (whose husband printed the plates) and Jacques Frélaut (who was Roger Lacourière's collaborator), and with the approval of the heirs, by the one hundred copper plates etched by Picasso, followed by Roger and Madeleine Lacourière's gift, in 1982, of the complete and unique series of the one hundred plates in their final state, each bearing the artist's handwritten "Bon à tirer" (final proof).

The print, being easy to reproduce and distribute in large numbers, is an effective means of political expression: to protest against Franco's coup d'état in 1937, Picasso printed two plates to accompany one of his poems, *Sue print, being easy to r* (Dream and Lie of Franco), which he then sold for the benefit of the Spanish Republic relief fund. In that same year, which also saw the creation of *Guernica,* he made a print called *The Weeping* Woman, whose tormented face denounces the horrors of war.

The post-war period was an especially fertile one for the lithograph, one of which is particularly famous for having been widely reproduced: the dove that appeared on the poster for the First World Peace Congress in 1949. As with his copper plate engravings, Picasso often reworked the lithographic stone, working through many successive states. A striking example of this is the lithograph of *The Bull,* which went through no less than eleven states, the treatment of the bull progressing in its transformations from a conventional representation to a stylized one composed of a few simple lines. More series followed: *David and Bathsheba, after Cranach the Elder,* through ten states between 1947 and 1949; the *Woman in an Armchair* in 1948; the *Women of Algiers, after Delacroix,* in 1955 (which also inspired a series of etchings in that same year).

Picasso also used lithography for his book illustrations, and notably for Reverdy's *Chants des morts,* published by Teriade in 1948, of which the original layout with gouaches by Picasso is in the museum's collection.

If the inspiration for Picasso's engravings, lithographs, and linocuts until the late Sixties involved a variety of subjects (portraits of Françoise, of their children, Claude and Paloma, and of Jacqueline; as well as still lifes, bacchanals, bullfight scenes - in particular the twenty-six aquatints of the *Tauromaquia* of 1957 - , and, as always, the painter and his model), it was the representation of erotic imagery, centered primarily around the artist's studio, that dominated the production of the last fifteen years of his life.

The hand-press, used by Picasso at La Californie (his villa at Cannes) to print his own plates, was given to the museum by the artist's heirs.

A few Technical Terms

Wood Engraving

The artist cuts into the wood block, leaving his design in relief to be inked and printed with a press.

Metal Engraving

Etching

A metal plate (usually copper) is coated with a layer of varnish into which the artist will carve his design with a pointed tool; the plate is then immersed in an acid bath that bites only into the areas where the metal has been exposed by the carving. The plate can then be inked (the ink settling into the hollows) for printing.

Engraving with a Burin or Drypoint

The artist carves his design directly into the plate using a pointed tool; this technique does not permit corrections.

Lithography

The artist draws on a stone with an oily ink. The parts left uncovered are prepared so that the printer's ink will take only on the design (the principle involved is the mutual repulsion of oil and water: the stone having been wet before being inked, the ink will be retained by the oily parts and not by those wet with water).

Linoleum Engraving

The technique is the same as for wood engraving, except that the support used is a block of linoleum, which is much easier to carve.

Monotype

No engraving process is involved here, just the direct printing of a design (which may be on a variety of supports: glass, canvas, zinc, etc.). This technique yields only one print, hence the term monotype.

Second floor

Room **8**   The Bathers

1927-1937

Nude on a White Background

1927

The rhythm of the arabesque is broken here by sharp angles and points - breasts, hands, right foot - which reinforce the aggressivity of this figure, with its stringy hair and long, menacing, vertical mouth, opened in a too-thy grin that bodes no good, echoing the dark slit gaping below. One of the feet is huge, as if it were in the foreground, while the arm holding what looks like a comb tapers to a point, as if it were in the distance. Because of these apparent differences of scale, and in spite of the flat treatment of the background, the figure seems to be distorted in space like a hallucination.

Metamorphosis II

1928,
Paris

Two slightly different sculptures, one in bronze and the other in plaster, bear a title that aptly defines the fate to which Picasso subjects the human form: *Metamorphosis.*

Nude on a White Background
Oil on canvas
130 x 97 cm

Metamorphosis II
Plaster original
23 x 18 x 11 cm

Large Bather
Oil on canvas
195 x 130 cm

Even if, despite the deformations and displacements, we manage to recognize the elements that constitute its anatomy (head and face with eyes, nose, and mouth, breasts, buttocks, arms, legs), the woman has lost all human appearance and has been transformed into a disquieting protozoan creature, a sort of blob whose substance seems to have gathered in a monstrous foot. These sculptures were executed directly after drawings made at Cannes during the preceding summer; Picasso filled an entire sketchbook with such biomorphic, sculptural figures, all in volume and characterized by hermaphroditic protuberances (phallus, breasts), representing nude bathers on the beach generally in the act of opening the door of a cabin.

Large Bather

May 26, 1929,
Paris

Starting in 1918, as Picasso began spending most of his summers at seaside resorts like Dinard, Juan-les-Pins, and Cannes, the motif of bathers became a perennial feature of his work. During two consecutive summers at Dinard - in 1928 and 1929 -, and back in Paris in between, he painted many beach scenes, often using small formats, with female figures whose bodies seem to be made up of rounded, pebble-like forms, or flat, angular shapes like cardboard cutouts; the more intimate parts of their anatomies are generally prominently displayed as they cavort with a beachball, or, in an obvious sexual metaphor, open the door of their cabin with a key. The giant, and rather disquieting, bather here seems to have

The Swimmer
Oil on canvas
130 x 162 cm

been roughly hewn out of a block of wood; with those three black holes for a face, her visible ribcage, and enormous arms raising a black veil, she evokes, more than anything else, the menacing image of death.

The Swimmer

November 1929,
Paris

Freed of its weight, this creature is floating in the water, limbs spread and stretched out in all directions; some seem to be quite precariously attached, like the hand that is about to break off from an arm. Picasso's imagination has created a sort of headless being, a life form that is all arms and legs; a foot, whose original rose color shows through the layer of blue paint, is partially visible in a reworked area on the right; what may be a head, indicated by a pair of nostrils, has been fused with one of the hands. The many traces of reworking show the considerable difficulty that the painter must have had in defining the shape of this odd creature.

Construction with Glove

August 22, 1930,
Juan-les-Pins

Between the 14th and 28th of August, while on holiday at Juan-les-Pins, Picasso made eight rather strange "relief pictures" (all of which belong to the museum): he took some small-format canvases, sometimes using the back (in which case the stretcher becomes a frame around the composition), onto which he glued or sewed all kinds of objects, probably found on the beach: pieces of vegetable matter, wood, cardboard, or abandoned toys, which he then covered with a layer of sand. There

Construction with Glove
Colored sand, glove, cardboard,
plant matter on canvas, 27. 5 x 35.5 x 8 cm

was nothing haphazard in the way in which these found objects were worked, cut, fashioned, and assembled into striking compositions that present images of a dreamlike quality (in creating a uniform color and texture, the sand adds to the unreality of these objects): a disembodied hand (in fact a glove filled with bran) has been placed here next to a strange head with bared teeth and dishevelled hair, like the remains of a being from a sunken world cast up on the sand by the sea.

Figures at the Seashore

January 12, 1931,
Paris

Blue sea, yellow sand, and cabins blazing white in the sun, on a beach that is deserted except for the presence of two beings that are locked in a convulsive, ferocious embrace, seemingly more intent on devouring each other than on kissing. The spherical breasts of the woman are visible, but nothing really distinguishes the man from the woman in this aggregate of flesh-colored, smooth, rounded forms that look like so many eroded pebbles. Most likely, the wo-

man's face is the one with closed eyelids which is about to be penetrated by the phallic nose of her partner, whose eyes - two black dots - seem to be open, while their pointed tongues dart between rows of menacing teeth. There is something phallic too about those disjointed limbs that clash together rather than intertwine. In this picture Picasso pushed his transposition of the human form to the limits of the bearable, creating an image charged with incredible aggressivity and sexual intensity. No realistic representation could ever have managed to convey such violence.

Bather

1931,
Boisgeloup

"Picasso worships this very first goddess of fertility, this quintessence of the female form, with a body that seems to have swollen and ripened like a fruit, as if charged by man's desire", wrote the photographer Brassaï, who had come across a cast of the Venus of Lespugue among the treasures that Picasso kept in his "museum" (a display cabinet in which Picasso stashed all sorts of

Figures at the Seashore
Oil on canvas
130 x 195 cm

Bather
Bronze
70 x 40.2 x 31.5 cm

little sculptures and objects). There is indeed an analogy to be made between the forms of the archaic goddess and those of this bather whose hypertrophied belly, breasts, and legs do not exclude a certain graceful movement. In fact, she is amazingly dynamic: the prominence of the forward-thrusting breasts, the torsion of the bust, and the curling of the arms, as much as the position of the legs, serve to create an impression of motion. A tiny insectile head with globular eyes tops this lumbering anatomy.

Woman in a Red Armchair

January 21, 1932,
Boisgeloup

For months Picasso had been working in plaster, bringing into being dazzling white sculptures with softly rounded forms that evoked the ripe body of his mistress, Marie-Thérèse. For months too, he had been preoccupied with the same forms in his paintings, involved as usual in the constant

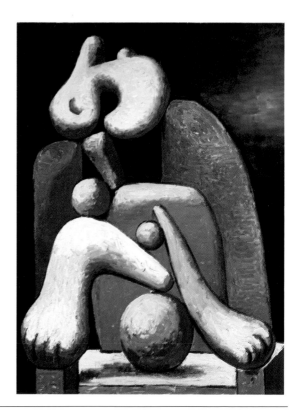

Woman in a Red Armchair
Oil on canvas
130.2 x 97 cm

Bather with a Book
Oil, pastel, and charcoal on canvas
130 x 97.5 cm

interplay between the various mediums that he used. A comparison with other canvases in which the model is more easily recognizable allows us to identify these forms as those of a Marie-Thérèse who is nonchalantly, pensively, or wearily slumped in a red armchair. Her body seems to be made of a heap of stones or bones ("I have a veritable passion for bones", Picasso once said) which stand, as autonomous elements, for the different parts of her anatomy: head, neck, torso with two little balls for the breasts, and club-like arms around the large ball of her abdomen. So unstable is this heap that the slightest displacement of one of its elements would send it tumbling. The stark lighting which makes the volumes stand out against the black, featureless background, lends a disquieting note to this inaccessible, stony figure.

Bather with a Book

February 18, 1937,
Paris

The first thing to notice in this picture is the rough and matte texture of the paint, which makes the body of the bather look as if it were made of pumice: Picasso used a mixture of oils and pastels for his paint. The rounded volumes that define the figure are, in some places, interrupted by large facets like a Cubist sculpture. The woman is reading a book, hunched over, resting her chin on he hands, her legs crossed under her. A small portion of blue sea is visible, indicating that she is on the beach, otherwise there is nothing to open up the small space which is entirely occupied by her monumental presence.

Room 9

Boisgeloup
The Sculptor's Studio

1930-1935

1930	June	Picasso buys the château de Boisgeloup, near Gisors.
1931		He works primarily on sculpture; his model seems to be Marie-Thérèse.
1932	June-July	First retrospective exhibition - composed of 236 works chosen by Picasso - at the Galerie Georges Petit in Paris.
	October	Christian Zervos publishes the first volume of his catalogue of Picasso's work (33 volumes in all will be published by 1978).
1933		Picasso works intensively on engraving.
	June 1	First issue of the magazine *Minotaure,* with cover by Picasso.
1935	Spring	Complete break with Olga, who leaves their rue La Boétie apartment with Paulo. Alone and disturbed by his problems, Picasso painted little and turned to writing poems ("the worst period of my life", he later remarked).
	July	Picasso asks his old friend Sabartés, then living in South America, to return and become his secretary.
	September 5	Birth of a daughter to Picasso and Marie-Thérèse : Maria de la Concepción, nicknamed Maya.

Boisgeloup,
sculptures in the studio,
around 1933
(Archives Picasso,
photo: Bernés-Marouteau)

Seated or Standing Women

1930, Boisgeloup

Picasso pointed out that it was with "a little knife", not exactly the sculptor's noblest tool, that he carved these small hieratic female figures, out of a no-less humble material: some very ordinary pinewood that must have been lying around his studio or that he must have found who knows where. The long and slender forms of the figurines were probably determined by the shape of the pieces of wood; fated to be vertical, they cannot even free their arms from their bodies (the arms of the one figure that has managed to do so are additions). In spite of the visible marks of the carving tool, there is nothing crude about these figures which were cut and shaped with great dexterity and daring; they are, in fact, not without a certain elegance, a fragile and an archaic grace (Malraux called them "Cretan women", alluding to the art of the ancient Mediterranean; they have also justifiably been compared to small Etruscan bronzes). Some of them feature the profile of Marie-Thérèse, Picasso's young mistress.

Still Life on a Pedestal Table

March 11, 1931, Paris

"This is some still life!", Picasso remarked many years later, standing in front of this monumental canvas which is endowed with a powerful, vital energy by the insistent play of curvilinear forms (even the wainscot is swept up by the swirling rhythm) that seem to be breathing, swelling up, twisting, and stretching out, from the feet of the table to the handle of the pitcher, as vivacious as plants, in a bright color scheme that further enhances the impression of overflowing energy. The painter's words take on their full significance when we realize that this work has a hidden meaning: pointing to the sinuous lines and vaguely anthropomorphic forms, he revealed the suggested presence of the beautiful, curvaceous body of the young Marie-Thérèse, with whom he had been secretly involved for several years at the time. Transposing the representation of her body into a series of rounded forms, which are so many images of fertility (the fruits, the belly of the pitcher), he was able to portray a reality that, without his explanation, few would ever have guessed.

Head of a Woman

1931, Boisgeloup

In June 1930, Picasso bought a 17th-century manor at Boisgeloup, a small village near Gisors, not far from Paris. The buildings of the château had the vast, empty spaces that he needed in order to - at last! - work comfortably on his sculptures. Abandoning metal, whose possibilities he had boldly explored with the help of González, he took up a more traditional material and technique: plaster modelling (he liked its whiteness; now lost because of the handling necessary for casting in bronze). In a few months he had already produced a large series of works modelled in the round, to use an especially appropriate expression. Endeavoring to represent the characteristic forms of the head of his model, Marie-Thérèse Walter, he isolated its main elements: her fine, straight hair, rounded eyes, large nose, prominent cheekbones, accentuating the volumes, turning them into organic forms - with rather obvious sexual connota-

Standing Woman
Sculpted pine
48 x 3 x 5 cm

Standing Woman
Sculpted pine,
metal wire
47.5 x 5 x 7.5 cm

Still Life on a Pedestal Table
Oil on canvas
195 x 130.5 cm

Head of a Woman
Plaster original
71.5 x 41 x 33 cm

Head of a Woman
Plaster original
128.5 x 54.5 x 62.5 cm

tions - which he then positioned as if they were movable elements (there are sketches around this type of sculpture in which the separate parts of the head are numbered and then put into place). This head is particularly striking for the bold deformations that make it seem as if there were several different faces when one moves around it.

Head of a Woman

1931,
Boisgeloup

Of all the heads of Marie-Thérèse sculpted at Boisgeloup, this one is the most monumental. It has retained the whiteness which Picasso was so fond of that he hesitated a long time before having it cast in bronze (this bronze is also in the museum's collection) many years later, during the war, at the insistence of his friend Sabartés, who was concerned about the fragility of the plaster. Here again, the head has been subjected to drastic deformations, in particular the protuberant, monolithic mass of the forehead-nose, an anatomical invention devised by the sculptor to represent one of the characteristic features of his model's face. It may have been influenced by the morphology of a mask from the Nimba tribe of Guinea that he had at Boisgeloup (today in the museum), and which presents the same protuberant nasal appendage. At the same time, this face presents classical features that recall the beauty of the sculpture of Antiquity: Greek profile, small mouth with parted lips, rounded chin. A cement version of this head (today in the museum at Antibes) was exhibited at the entrance to the Spanish Pavilion of the 1937 Paris World Fair.

The Sculptor
Oil on plywood
128.5 x 96 cm

The Sculptor

December 7, 1931,
Paris

In a studio whose depth is suggested by the receding lines of the floorboards, seated on a green marble cube, the curly-haired and bearded sculptor (seen in profile and frontal views), who is resting his chin on his hand, contemplates a female bust on its base (but the wide-opened eye makes the face seem so alive one wonders if it is really a sculpture). The bust has the easily recognizable features - forehead prolonged by the nose, rounded chin - of the artist's favorite model at the time, Marie-Thérèse Walter, whose presence came to prevail more and more in Picasso's work, attesting to a close relationship that had long been kept a secret. The theme of the sculptor in his studio - a reflection of Picasso's own activity during the early Thirties - was extensively developed in a series of etchings included in the *Suite Vollard:* the main figures are those of the artist, who has the serenity of an antique god, and of his model, who has the beautiful face and graceful body of the woman he loves, represented either as a woman in the flesh, or as a statue, like the work of a new Pygmalion.

Seated Woman with a Book
Oil on canvas
130 x 97.5 cm

Seated Woman with a Book

January 2, 1932,
Boisgeloup

The presence of Marie-Thérèse in his life led Picasso to develop a new language of forms, the figure being simplified and reduced to a series of rounded volumes, just like the three-dimensional representations, in relief or in the round, that he made of her at the time. He accentuated the characteristic features of a face that was already naturally sculptural: the nose merges with the forehead, the eyes are very distinctly shaped, the cheekbones prominent; the face is shown simultaneously in frontal and profile views, while the contrast between the violet and green increases the impression of volume in the ball-shaped head. The curves of the armchair and the sinuous lines of the clothing (the belt buckle and the wood panelling of the walls are the only true rectilinear elements) add their undulating rhythm to the curvaceous figure.

Sleeping Nude

April 4, 1932,
Boisgeloup

Marie-Thérèse asleep. As plant-like as the leaves that she nonchalantly holds or the pears that lie next to her knee, she has become a sort of human still life: the lush forms of her body are as full as a ripe fruit; or almost ripe, a ripening fruit with firm skin and a slightly sour flavor like those of the green and red apples evoked by her breasts. There is also the presentiment of a future happy event (Maya, the daughter of Picasso and Marie-Thérèse, will be born in 1935), suggested by the sleeping face which seems to be nestled in the protective obscurity of a uterine pocket. The amorous painter took great pleasure in exaggerating the roundness of the youthful figure of his blond mistress, the voluptuous pose of her body displaying its charms as she sleeps. The brightness of the color scheme describes, again in hyperbolic terms, the luminosity of her skin, which is almost dazzling in the light of the sun. From this radiant apparition seem to be emanating waves - of light or of pleasure - that merge into the pattern of the wallpaper in the background. Never before had Picasso depicted with such enthusiasm the sensual attraction, the trusting tenderness, and the fascination (to the point of obsession, so present is Marie-Thérèse in his work) that are the lot of happy lovers.

Sleeping Nude
Oil on canvas
130 x 161.7 cm

Composition with Butterfly

September 15, 1932,
Boisgeloup
Acquired in 1982

André Breton said that when he saw this composition, he felt as if he were in the presence of a revelation, so intense was his emotion before the perfection of this amazing image of reality merging with the imaginary: a suspended instant, an ephemeral moment of life caught in the web of the canvas just like the butterfly itself, a Pieris Rapae, snared by a tangle of twigs (although it seems that it could fly away at any moment), next to a beech leaf that is so dry that only a diaphanous network of filaments remains, between two little figures, one of which is made of twigs (or a frayed piece of hemp), and the other of matches, cloth, and a thumbtack (for the head), which are probably, in spite of their coarse appearance, bathers playing on the beach. A milky-colored, enamel-like paint gives a protective coat to these fragile objects. The

Composition with Butterfly
Material, wood, vegetable matter, string,
thumbtack, butterfly, oil on canvas
16 x 22 x 2.5 cm

impression of timelessness in this scene is offset, however, by the sense of a slow disintegration suggested by the frayed piece of cloth, the decomposed leaf, the undone rope. The date has been marked in the paint itself: "Boisgeloup 15 septembre XXXII".

Nude in a Garden
Oil on canvas
162 x 130 cm

Nude in a Garden

August 4, 1934,
Boisgeloup

A wood-nymph, all in shades of pink, nestling in luxuriant green vegetation; a sleeping odalisque resting her head on a rich oriental-style cushion embroidered in gold: Marie-Thérèse abandons herself to sleep (for Picasso she will always be the woman who sleeps), displaying simultaneously, impossibly, all of her most secret charms in a topology of promised pleasures. She has the somewhat swollen neck of Ingres's bathers, and the same serene impudicity, and yet also, with her closed eyes, a certain innocence.

Woman Reading

January 9, 1935,
Paris

A female figure seated in a chair reads a book placed on a table in front of a window; the knob silhouetted against the pane is a recurrent motif in the many interior scenes painted during this period. In all likelihood the reader is Marie-Thérèse, although the rigid and angular contours of her body here are at the opposite extreme of the rounded volumes that usually served to represent her. The same harshness is to be seen in the rest of the picture, which is dominated by triangular forms set off by black outlines like the leaded panes of stained glass windows. This strong geometrization of the forms - her hands look like knife blades - detracts from the apparent serenity of the scene, and even gives it a disquieting aspect.

Woman Reading
Oil on canvas
162 x 113 cm

Room 10   The Crucifixion
The Corrida
Minotauromachy

The Crucifixion

February 7, 1930
Paris

Our initial reaction may well be one of surprise at the unexpected presence in Picasso's work of a religious subject, and even more so because of the formal and chromatic violence (not the violence of provocation, but that of the primitive energy of the sacred) with which he treated this scene of the Crucifixion. It was not the first time that he handled this theme; he would return to it two years later in drawings inspired by the Isenheim Altarpiece of Matthias Grünewald, and then again in the Fifties in juxtaposition with the theme of the corrida.

The iconography here is very difficult to decipher, Picasso having introduced into this episode of the Passion some demonic creatures from his own universe, with their particular emotional charge. In the middle is the Christ, a colorless, round-headed figure clad in a long loincloth like his Romanesque counterparts, set off against the darkness that has fallen on the world; a small red figure perched on a disproportionately tall ladder is nailing him to the cross (unless he is doing the opposite, for the ladder is generally to be found in Deposition scenes); an even tinier figure on horseback (like a picador), completely out of scale with the rest of the scene, is piercing Christ's side with a spear, which a disheveled woman with bared teeth seems to be about to bite into (is it a figure of the Virgin, as is generally believed? Or could it be the Magdalen, who is usually shown kissing the Christ's feet?). To the left of the figure on horseback, there is a monstrous, open-mouthed giant wearing a purple cloak, onto whose back a bird seems to have fallen, struck by a large stone above (which

The Crucifixion
Oil on plywood
51.5 x 66.5 cm

Woman with Stiletto
Oil on canvas
46.5 x 61.5 cm

may be one of the attributes of the Passion: the sponge soaked in vinegar offered to the Christ to slake his thirst).

The two dislocated bodies at the foot of the ladder must be those of the two thieves, whose T-shaped crosses, one red and one yellow, stand at opposite ends of the picture. In the foreground, two Roman soldiers are playing dice on a drum (which recalls those of the saltimbanque period) for the seamless cloak of Christ, which is being held by the helmeted figure on the left. A few figures on the right are more difficult to make out and identify: under Christ's arm seems to be the profile of Marie-Thérèse, outlined in red against a yellow triangle; next to this is a wild-haired solar figure, and below, in blue and white, there is what can be identified, thanks to comparisons with other paintings, as a woman's head with mandibles very much like those of a praying mantis, and which may belong to the two yellow arms raised to the sky in a gesture of lamentation.

Woman with Stiletto
(The Death of Marat)

December 19-25, 1931,
[Paris]

When he represented the death of Marat, David showed the French revolutionary lying inert in his bathtub, still holding the quill with which he had been writing and the request addressed to him by his assassin, Charlotte Corday. Picasso, haunted as he was by representations of cruelty in the midst of conflicts in his personal life, remembered this episode of a power struggle in which a man falls victim to a woman. In what mortal danger did he feel himself to be, that he had to exorcise it with an image such as this? His Charlotte Corday is a nude, dishevelled, sadistic, shrieking figure who is stabbing a frail, sexless Marat, above whose head her gaping, tooth-ridden mouth hovers like some latter-day crown of thorns. In between them, a French flag underscores the historical reference. There is blood everywhere, spreading on the floor and walls like a substance with a life of its own. In the cramped space (further constricted by the accelerated perspective) in which this nightmarish scene is taking place, the misshapen bodies seem to be about to change even more: the victim's body deflating like a punctured balloon, while that of his assassin, which is still emerging from the menacing space behind the door, seems to be ready to swell up even more. There is no telling how far this horror will go.

Bullfight: The Death of the Female Torero
Oil and pencil on wood
21.7 x 27 cm

Bullfight: The Death of the Female Torero

September 6, 1933,
Boisgeloup

The great Spanish theme of the bullfight is present throughout Picasso's work. What he was attracted to in this spectacle was less its picturesque aspects - the sundrenched arenas, the ballet of the toreros, the shimmering colors of their "costume of light" - than the slow ritual of death, the dangerous and ruthless confrontation of man and beast. In this picture the bull overwhelms the arena with its impetuous presence, a perfect image of the untamable brute beast that it is. In an assault that resembles a rape, it has gored the fear-crazed horse, which throws its head back in agony (the bull and dying horse will reappear in *Guernica*, four years later). The inherent eroticism of this scene is reinforced by the presence of the half-dismounted female torero, whose body denuded by the force of the charge and lies in an attitude of abandon that could mean love, or death. Once more, this woman is none other than Marie-Thérèse.

Woman with Leaves

1934,
Boisgeloup

One of the things that Picasso liked to do was "to make something out of anything"... A matchbox, fallen leaves, a piece of corrugated cardboard, some of the many objects found and gathered here and there

Woman with Leaves
Bronze
37.9 x 20 x 25.9 cm

The Minotauromachy
Aquatint and scraper
49.8 x 69.3 cm

which he carefully kept in his studio - because they could always be good for something… His inventive genius as a sculptor brought them together in an unexpected fashion thanks to a technique that he often used in his sculpture of those years: imprints of their shape or texture were made directly in the plaster with which he modelled the little figure: the matchbox became the face, the corrugated texture of the cardboard gave shape to the elegant folds of the garment which drapes this female figure like an antique priestess. The beech leaves, whose fine details have been retained, contribute a feeling of life to this small, yet monumental figure so beautiful and mysterious, despite the incongruity of the materials of which it was made.

Minotauromachy

1935

The Minotaur is undoubtedly the most fascinating symbolic figure in Picasso's work of the early Thirties, where it occupies a prominent position, especially in his drawings and prints (and in particular in the *Suite Vollard*). Like the tragic creature in the ancient myth (born of the unholy union of a woman and a bull, it was condemned to live in the labyrinth built by Daedalus, where it devoured youths and maidens offered in sacrifice until it was slain by Theseus, who found his way out thanks to Ariadne's thread), the Minotaur, half-man and half-beast, was at the mercy of his brutal instincts, a fitting image of the painful duality of the human condition. His fate here is no less sad: drunk with wine from libations, he rapes the terror-stricken women; thrown into the arena for the amusement of the young girls, he is wounded and then put to death like the bull in a corrida; blind and helpless, he lets himself be led by a little girl. The latter reappears in an etching of *Minotauromachy* (an appropriate title to express the intertwining of the two themes of the Minotaur and of the Bullfight) in which she faces the beast with a lighted candle in one hand, and a bouquet in the other; between them there is the disembowelled horse with the bare-breasted female torero on its back, who could be dead or turning her sword on herself, under the gaze of two young girls at a window, while a bearded man tries to escape by climbing a ladder (not unlike the one of the *Crucifixion*). A product of Picasso's personal mythology, this strange scene is just as full of enigmas as it is of clues; its symbolic significance is only partially decipherable (life and death, war and peace, light and darkness, innocence and bestiality).

Room 11 Women at Their Toilette

1938

Women at Their Toilette

1938
Paris

Almost 3 m. high and 4.50 m. wide, this gigantic *papier collé* was originally a cartoon for a tapestry that could not be executed at the time; it was woven thirty years later at the Gobelins manufactory, at the behest of André Malraux. A woman sitting crosslegged on the floor is having her hair combed by another woman, while a third is holding a mirror for her; on the left, a vase of flowers stands on a pedestal table. On a beige-colored ground, which is still visible in some spots, Picasso pasted pieces of patterned wallpaper and paper that he probably painted himself (yellows, blues, and whites). As was often the case with the Cubist collages, the patterned paper, which acts as a colored surface, sometimes imitates what it is supposed to represent: imitating wood for the floorboards and mirror frame, brick or stone for the wall in the background, and even the pink color of the skin of the seated woman, who wears little clothing, while her companions, on the other hand, have clothes made of decorative paper. The pieces of paper were cut either with straight contours, like Cubist forms, or torn into small pieces that were then pasted one on top of the other, leaving the torn edges visible, as if Picasso wanted to animate these large colored surfaces, as the painter can by leaving visible brushstrokes. Only the black areas were painted directly, probably in gouache, adding a painterly effect which contrasts with the precise aspect of the printed papers.

Women at their Toilette
Pasted wallpaper and gouache on mounted paper
299 x 448 cm

Room **12**   The Sculpture Garden

Woman in a Garden
welded and painted steel
206 x 117 x 85 cm

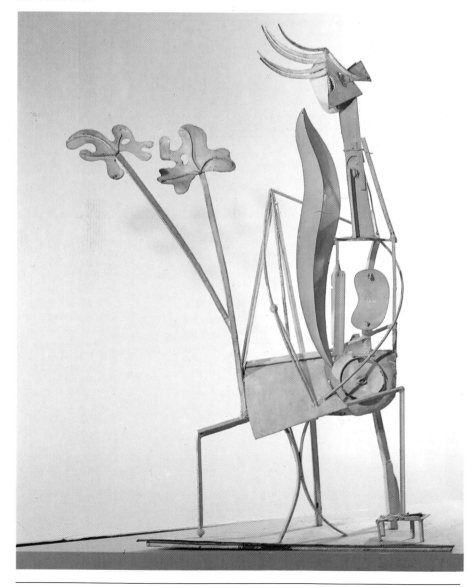

Woman in a Garden

1930-1931,
Paris

According to the sculptor González, in whose studio it was made (as were the metal wire constructions of 1928), Picasso spent many months working on this sculpture, and with particular care, for it was originally intended as a monument in homage to Guillaume Apollinaire. The coat of white paint harmonizes the varied bits and pieces of metal - cut sheet metal, steel bars of different shapes, nails, objects (manufactured, but hardly identifiable), forged pieces - that Picasso is said to have assembled himself (which would explain certain technical imperfections). The figure presents iconographical analogies with those painted in pictures during the same period: pointed female head with peduncular eyes, tooth-ridden mouth, sharp-edged hair, and flowing, plantlike forms (there was a philodendron in the apartment on rue La Boétie). The parts cut out of sheet metal were probably made by González after drawings provided by Picasso (the woman's head, the leaves of the plant, the table); these well-shaped pieces contrast with the rough aspect of the improvised materials. The whole is a rhythmic assemblage of lines and planes interwoven with space.

Woman with an Orange
Bronze
180.5 x 75 x 67.5 cm

Woman with an Orange

1934,
Boisgeloup

This is the largest figure that Picasso made using the technique of pressing shapes and textures into plaster. The rectangular cover of a box must have served to make the head, holes were then made for the eyes, and a nose added; the tubular neck emerges from a ruffled collar made by the impression of a cake mold in the plaster; a roll of corrugated cardboard gave its shape to the bust, which looks like a fluted column, and which was set on a "skirt" that was textured with chicken wire. Two extremely long arms (part of which were made of wood in the original plaster model) were grafted onto the thin body, and at the end of one of these is a sort of hand with a ball (the orange), while the other holds a vase that looks like a hotwater bottle. The broad movement of her arms (in a gesture that is not without analogy to Eve's tempting offer), at least as much as her stature, gives her an imposing and a solemn presence.

Woman with a Push Chair

1950,
Vallauris

The imprints of many different objects were made in plaster to compose this sculpture, but our perception of their assemblage is considerably altered by the fact of its "translation" into bronze. Nevertheless, a closer look permits us to identify the various materials used: a patched-up baby carriage (of which only one of the wheels is

Woman with a Push Chair
Bronze
203 x 145 x 61 cm

original), pieces of pottery (the head and limbs of the baby; the mother's skirt, made with a special tile used in ceramics to hold wares in the kiln for firing), iron stove plates for the corsage, and cake pans for the breasts. The eye takes pleasure in recognizing these commonplace objects, to replace this sculpture back in a more familiar sphere; in the same way, its subject alludes to Picasso's everyday life, since, at the time, he often took his children Paloma and Claude (aged respectively one and three years old) to the beach in a stroller. The bizarre humor of the assemblage is also present in its forms: the baby's bow-legs, the stove-pipe silhouette of the woman in her high-heels, and the long neck topped by a tiny, insectile head.

Room 13 The Muses

1936-1937

1936		Ties of friendship develop between Picasso and Paul Eluard, one of the poets of the Surrealist group. Through Eluard he meets Dora Maar, a young photographer, who will become his mistress.
	February 18	Victory of the Popular Front in Spain.
	July 18	Outbreak of civil war in Spain.
1937	January	Finds new studio at 7, rue des Grands-Augustins. The Spanish Republican government commissions Picasso to paint a mural for the Spanish Pavilion at the World Fair to be held in Paris at the beginning of the summer: the future *Guernica*.

Valentine Penrose, Nusch Eluard, Dora Maar, a friend,
Paul Eluard, Lise Deharme, and Picasso at Saint-Tropez in 1936
(Archives Picasso, photo: R. Penrose)

The Straw Hat with Blue Leaves
Oil on canvas
61 x 50 cm

The Straw Hat with Blue Leaves

May 1, 1936,
Juan-les-Pins

It is hard to tell if the subject here is a still life or a woman's face. Eyes haphazardly placed at the edges of a fleshy form that also features a nose, with well-defined nostrils seen from below, and a gaping mouth. This face seems to float in front of a purplish neck - which looks very much like a vase -, on top of which rests a straw hat in the shape of a figure-eight decorated with blue leaves. Below the neck is a collarlike affair, that could just as well be the edge of a small table; and below that, very crudely delineated breasts. All of these dislocated forms, along with the ambiguity, make for a rather disturbing, even somewhat obscene picture.

Portrait of Dora Maar

1937,
[Paris]

The new woman in Picasso's life as of 1936, a young photographer associated with the Surrealists, Dora Maar, soon made her appearance in his work in a series of portraits that alternated with those of Marie-Thérèse. We see that her hair was as dark as Marie-Thérèse's was fair; she is elegantly dressed in a black blouse decorated with brightly colored embroidery and a checked skirt, and looks sophisticated right down to the tips of her polished fingernails. The resemblance with the model and the sort of psychological equivalent of it that can be achieved in paint result from a series of formal and chromatic transpositions. The face has been shown in frontal and profile views; the eyes, also shown from different angles, have a lively expression because of their different colors, red and green. The juxtaposition of so many colors here - mauve, yellow, green, and pink - has been made with such skill that we forget its improbability, while it also renders the luminous quality of the sitter's complexion. The bright color scheme - with a dominant opposition of red and black - and the angularity of the forms - fingernails, elbow - give the impression that she must have been a temperamental woman, one who, according to Brassaï, "was inclined to storms". As if Picasso were trying to keep her prisoner, she was represented in a strange decor with stripes, in a space that would have seemed even more confining had it not been painted white.

Portrait of Marie-Thérèse

January 6, 1937,
[Paris]

The vivacity of the dark-haired Dora was counter-balanced by the nonchalance of the blond Marie-Thérèse, the angular lines in the portrait of the one by the rounded contours in the portrait of the other: the gentle curves of the hat brim, the face, the movement of the arms, the breasts, and the fingertips with their short nails. The bright colors in Dora's portrait have given way here to pastel tones, predominantly in the blues and yellows. The comparison of these two women through their portraits gives a good idea of the contrast in their personalities and an even clearer idea of the painter's vision of them; rarely has painting succeeded in being so "psychological", all the while bypassing realistic representation.

Portrait of Dora Maar
Oil on canvas
92 x 65 cm

Portrait of Marie-Thérèse
Oil on canvas
100 x 81 cm

Weeping Woman

October 18, 1937,
Paris

This weeping figure is related to the women in *Guernica:* the mother holding her child, the despair-stricken woman before the burning house. In the months that followed the execution of his great mural, this motif kept appearing, like an obssessive theme, in Picasso's drawings, paintings, and engravings. In this picture the image has been extremely simplified: there are no more jagged tears in the corners of the eyes, the mouth no longer bares its teeth in a rictus. The woman, who is dressed in black, holds a handkerchief to her face, which seems to be covered with a maze of lines, furrows etched, as if by team, into the very thickness of the paint. In this grief-stricken face the eyes themselves have become two big tears. The figure of the weeping woman is traditionally interpreted as being Dora Maar, about whom Picasso reportedly said: "I have never been able to see, or imagine her otherwise than in tears."

Maya with a Doll

January 16, 1938,
Paris

Maya, the daughter of Picasso and Marie-Thérèse, was born on September 5, 1935. The presence of this little pig-tailed girl is a discreet one in Picasso's work (his liaison with Marie-Thérèse and the birth of Maya were known to few people at the time, and he never really lived with them). But whenever she does appear, as a baby at her mother's breast or as a little girl playing, we can sense the affectionate and sympathetic attention that Picasso had for little children. Of course, he did not hesitate to deform her face, which is shown in frontal and profile views, yet the likeness remains, and with it an impression of life. Only the doll, an inanimate object, has the nose and eyes in the right place.

Portrait of Nusch Eluard

[Autumn] 1937,
Paris
1990 Dation

Picasso painted a radiant portrait of Nusch, the wife of his friend, the poet Paul Eluard, whose beauty we also know from Man

Weeping Woman
Oil on canvas
55.3 x 46.3 cm

Maya with a Doll
Oil on canvas
73.5 x 60 cm

Portrait of Nusch Eluard
Oil on canvas
92 x 62.5 cm

Ray's photographs. There is something mysterious and fragile in the elongated eyes and thin lips. The face, which is divided between night and day, yellow and blue, sunlight and moonshine, shown in both frontal and profile views, with its ethereal nimbus of hair, reveals the young woman's sensitivity. The distortions introduced by the painter do not affect the resemblance of the portrait. Picasso played on the elegance of his model's apparel, which is highlighted by the glossy paint he used: hat worn tilted frontwards in the pre-war style, double-breasted overcoat with large buttons and wide, stand-off collar. The two brooches depicting cupids on the lapels were made by Jean Schlumberger for the designer Elsa Schiaparelli; one holds a holding torch - the light of life - while the other seems to hold a tambourin which looks more like a skull, a premonitory symbol of Nusch's untimely death in 1946.

Room 14 Ceramics

A painter, sculptor, and engraver, Picasso was also a ceramist. What led him to embrace this new vocation was his encounter in 1946 with Suzanne and Georges Ramié, who ran the Madoura pottery works in Vallauris. The word vocation here is not too stong: Picasso turned to this new craft with his usual enthusiasm and curiosity, explored all its possibilities, and produced a large number of works. Here too, he overturned established practices, adopting the most unorthodox, even heretical techniques: "An apprentice who worked like Picasso would never find a job", the Ramiés often remarked.

Picasso at Vallauris, September 1952
(Documentation du musée Picasso, photo: R. Doisneau)

Kiln stilt decorated with a child holding a dove
Autumn 1950
Red clay, painted with slips
59 x 23 x 7.5 cm

Piece of Brick with Face of a Woman
12 July 1962
White clay, painted with slips
22 x 7.5 x 13

The Supports

As supports for his decoration, Picasso often used traditional wares - plates, dishes, vases - of the kind standardly produced at the Madoura pottery. He also used more mass-produced objects like cooking vessels and tiles of all kinds, or, of course, whatever happened to be at hand: this included accessories used to hold pieces placed in the kilns for firing (like these large tiles with triangular holes called stilts), not to mention all sorts of discarded bits and pieces of pottery and bricks, which, with a few dabs of color, he transformed into faces with all manner of delightful expressions.

Often, Picasso fashioned the pieces himself, proceeding less as a ceramist than as a sculptor, approaching the clay as if it were just another material like wood, plaster, or metal, to model figurines of nymphs, satyrs, and other pastoral figures. More frequently, however, he reworked forms that had already been turned on the potter's wheel or pressed in molds at the Madoura workshop; while the clay was still wet and malleable, he performed the most varied operations to bring about astonishing transformations: from vases and bottles, he created little female figures that have been called "tanagras" because of their resemblance to these ancient statuettes, and also puff-cheeked heads, or vases filled with flowers, as well as birds, pigeons, and doves.

Bottle: Woman Kneeling
[1950]
White clay, oxides painted on white enamel
29 x 17 x 17 cm

Vase: Woman with a Mantilla
[1949]
White clay, painted with slips
47 x 12.5 x 9.5 cm

The Decoration

Unlike the colors of the painter, which are immediately visible, those of the ceramist appear only upon firing, which means that a certain amount of experience is necessary in order to visualize the result beforehand and to pick the necessary colors accordingly. Most likely Picasso proceeded empirically, mixing all the different elements available: metal oxide, slip (color with a liquid clay base), enamel, pastel, glazes, patinas. To these he sometimes added incongruous and unorthodox materials: slag, or terracotta debris that served to make the horns and beards of grinning satyrs decorating the bottoms of plates. Working directly in the soft clay, he cut, scraped, and carved, combining incised and painted

Angry Owl
1947-1953
White clay, cast in a mold,
painted with slips
28. 5 x 30 x 32 cm

Spanish Dish with an Eye and Bulls
20 May 1957
Red clay, painted with slips, engraved and partly
glazed with brush
Ø 40 cm

Cooking pot with a She Goat and Head
and Bust of a Man Holding a Cup
5 August 1950
Red culinary clay, painted with black slip
19.7 x 27 x 24.5 cm

motifs. These bold and inventive practices gave rise to works that may, at times, have disconcerted amateurs of traditional ceramics (who didn't fail to point out when a glaze had retracted, or when a metal oxide had been fired too long!), but they had the beauty and charm of the unexpected. It was in these works that Picasso's Mediterranean roots revealed themselves most fully: ceramic pottery is an ancient technique (Picasso made direct reference to this when he decorated ocher-colored pots with black paint, as the Greeks had done long before), and very naturally a certain repertoire of motifs came into being in his works: satyrs, flute players, laurel-crowned dancers, and tumble-bellied sileni with their processions of bacchanalian revellers. And everywhere, the owl, emblem of Athena, and the bull - the toro of the corrida rather than the Cretan Minotaur -, two of the artist's favorite animals.

All of the works displayed here are one-of-a-kind pieces. Others were produced in limited editions at the Madoura pottery from a model made by Picasso (these bear the seal "Edition", or "Empreinte originale").

Salle **15** From Guernica to the War

1937-1939

1937	April 27	German aviation bombs the small Basque town of Guernica for over three hours. This senseless massacre of a civilian population shocks and outrages the world.
	May 1	Picasso draws the first sketches for the mural that he has accepted to make for the Spanish Pavilion at the Paris World Fair: his subject was inspired by the recent event: burning city, grief-stricken women, disemboweled horse, dead soldier. In *Guernica*, Picasso expressed his "horror of the military caste which has drowned Spain in an ocean of sorrow and death". More than fifty studies were executed around the large painting, which was completed in early June.
	July 12	Inauguration of the Spanish Pavilion.
1939	January 13	Death of Picasso's mother.
	September 1	Leaves for Royan with Dora, Sabartés and his wife. Marie-Thérèse and Maya are already there. Picasso will stay until the summer of 1941, occasionally making short trips to Paris.
	September 3	France enters the war.
	November	Large retrospective exhibition at the Museum of Modern Art in New York.

Guernica installed in the Spanish Pavilion
of the Paris World Fair, 1937
(Archives Picasso, photo: Kollar)

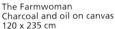
The Artist before His Canvas
Charcoal on canvas
130 x 94 cm

The Artist before His Canvas

March 22, 1938,
Paris

Picasso had not painted a self-portrait since 1921. In this one, he represented himself in the act of painting, wearing the striped sailor's shirt that he liked to affect in his stu-

dio. The face is shown - as usual, one is tempted to say - in frontal and in profile views. Some parts, like the arm and hand holding the palette, bear traces of reworking. The face was partially erased one day by the photographer David Douglas Duncan, who, in dusting the painting before taking a picture, removed some of the precious charcoal underdrawing that the artist had left unprotected.

The Farmwoman

March 23, 1938,
Paris

The enormous figure of a nude woman lying in a farmyard, with around her a hen, some chicks, and a rooster pecking grain (the rooster was one of the artist's obsessive motifs at the time). It is difficult to distinguish the woman's body from the elements of the background (although some parts touched up with pink paint help us to follow the form): the pile of compost behind her looks like it could be one of her legs, swollen and folded. This shamelessly displayed body with its wilted, sagging charms is anything but a beautiful sight; it is more of a flayed anatomy, as are the bodies of certain figures in *Guernica* whose muscles and tendons are visible. The smudgy, soiled aspect of the canvas as a whole contributes to the unpleasant impression created by its strange imagery: just what is this woman doing wallowing in the filth of a farmyard?

The Farmwoman
Charcoal and oil on canvas
120 x 235 cm

Man with a Straw Hat
and Ice Cream Cone
Oil on canvas
61 x 46 cm

Cat Catching a Bird
Oil on canvas
81 x 100 cm

Man with a Straw Hat and Ice Cream Cone

August 30, 1938,
Mougins

At Mougins that summer ice cream cones and lollipops were the rage: "Everybody - men, women, and children -, everybody was walking around licking something," Dora Maar recalled. This inspired Picasso to paint a series of very aggressive heads: here, the ice cream-eater is all in blue with yellow eyes, standing out against a black background. He looks like some kind of cactus-man; everything about him is prickly: his frayed straw hat, his hair, his eyelashes, his beard, the torn neck of his shirt, and even his tongue that darts greedily from his toothy mouth.

Catching a Bird

April 22, 1939,
Paris

In Spain, the last Republican strongholds had fallen into Franco's hands: Barcelona in January, Madrid and Valencia two months later. On March 15, Hitler marched into Prague and annexed Czechoslovakia. The death of Picasso's mother at the beginning of the year compounded with grief the anxiety caused by these political events. If themes of violence and death appeared in Picasso's work at this time, they may well have been provoked by this accumulation of misfortunes; there is no need to search for any particular symbolic significance. Yet what more universal image of the everyday reality of blind violence wreaked upon the weak and innocent, of the power of might over right, than this horrible, mud-caked creature (sand mixed in the paint) with fiendish eyes, clutching in its mouth a helpless bird that is struggling pathetically to fly away: "The subject just obsessed me, I don't know why," the painter once remarked.

Room **16** The Occupation and the Liberation

1940-1947

1941	August 25	Picasso returns to Paris. He lives in his studio on the rue des Grands-Augustins, where he works on sculpture again.
1942	June	Vlaminck attacks Picasso in *Comœdia:* "Picasso is guilty of having led French painting into a most fatal impasse".
	September 20	First issue of *Les Lettres françaises,* a clandestine publication by intellectuals of the Resistance.
1943	May	Picasso meets Françoise Gilot, with whom he will live for ten years.
1944	October 4	Announcement in *L'Humanité* that Picasso has joined the Communist Party.
	October	The exhibition of seventy-four paintings and five sculptures by Picasso at the Salon d'automne (called the Salon de la Libération that year) provokes violent demonstrations against both his work and his political involvement. This was the first time that he exhibited his work at a Salon.
1945	Autumn	Picasso begins to work on lithography in Mourlot's workshop in Paris.
1946	August	The curator of the Antibes museum, Dor de la Souchère, offers Picasso space to work in the museum: by November, he will have completed some twenty large panels on Mediterranean themes that will remain there. The museum will be renamed after Picasso. Publication of Sabartés's *Picasso: Portraits et souvenirs.*
1947	May	Picasso donates 10 of his paintings to the Musée National d'Art Moderne in Paris.

Seated Woman with a Hat
Oil on canvas
81 x 54 cm

Head of a Woman
Oil on canvas
65.5 x 54.5 cm

Seated Woman with Hat

May 27, 1939,
Paris

Can this prematurely aged woman be the blonde Marie-Thérèse? Everything is angular here: the chair, the wrinkles of the face (some of which were scratched into the thickness of the paint), the planes of the cheeks and chin. The worry-lines on the forehead, the baggy eyes, tired features, unsmiling mouth, and glazed expression give the feeling of a sort of stupor, which the bright colors and light background do little to relieve.

Head of a Woman

October 4, 1939,
Royan

A real hang-dog face. Picasso once said jokingly that his favorite models during the war were Dora Maar and his dog Kazbek, an Afghan hound that he took with him to Royan. Indeed, the forms of this head look more like a dog's muzzle and floppy ears

than the features of the beautiful woman, which Picasso "worked over" until he created this woodlike assemblage. The eyes are two dirty spots of paint, the mouth, gaping vertically, is sexually suggestive, but with her greyish skin and hair, she seems to be in mourning.

Woman with a Hat

June 9, 1941,
Paris

Brutal hands have fashioned this face, setting the eyes, nose, and forehead on one side, and the mouth, cheeks, and chin on the other, while at the junction of these two fragments of a human face, the nostrils have been stretched and twisted out of shape. These deformations are all the more unbearable because of the presence of realistic elements, like the last traces of something beautiful that has fallen apart. As if she were suffering from the effects of this mistreatment, Dora (recognizable by her nail-polished fingers) tightly grips the arms of her rigid and inhospitable-looking chair.

Woman with a Hat
Oil on canvas
92 x 60 cm

Small Boy with a Crayfish

June 21, 1941,
Paris

The little boy triumphantly wields a crayfish taken from a dish in front of him that also contains a fish and a medusa (probably inspired by the market at Royan). He exults in this catch, brandishing it like a scepter, and just as proudly displays his penis below, all smiles with his dancing eyes and toothless mouth. And yet there is something sad about this distant cousin of the street urchins painted by Murillo: there is like a grey veil that soils the colors, deadens the pinks, blues, and whites (this has sometimes been called Picasso's "Grey Period"). This may be the dark shadow cast on his work by the war, which he never represented directly (not even in *Guernica)*: "I didn't paint the war because I am not the kind of painter who goes around, like a photographer, looking for a subject. But there is no doubt that the war exists in the paintings that I did at the time".

Small Boy with a Crayfish
Oil on canvas
130 x 97.3 cm

Head of a Bull
Original materials (bicycle seat and handlebars)
33.5 x 43.5 x 19 cm

Death's Head
Bronze and brass
25 x 21 x 31 cm

Head of a Bull

Spring 1942,
Paris

A leather bicycle seat (model called "L'inextensible") and a rusty old pair of handlebars; "In a flash, they became associated in my mind", recalled this artist-wizard who had the power to give life to the humblest objects, transmuting them through the magic of his inventive genius. Assembled and cast in bronze, these scrapped bicycle parts became this amazingly evocative head of a bull, as if these two objects had always existed only to come together in this surprising configuration. All the while insisting upon the necessity of the encounter between these two objects, Picasso thought that they could regain their freedom and mused about a reverse metamorphosis, in which a passerby finding a bull's head in the street would think of using it to make a bicycle seat and handlebars.

Death's Head

1943,
Paris

This frightening visage of death seems to have come from an ossuary out of the depths of time, or some bone-heap left by the war still raging all around. To be sure, this motif, which he also represented in his paintings at the time, was related to contemporary events, but it also has a more universal meaning and belongs to the long line of meditations on this theme in Western funerary sculpture. The few details - eyesockets, nose cavity, barely visible clenched teeth - suffice to give it an amazingly realistic presence. The polished bronze makes it look like a stone eroded through the ages, gradually losing all trace of humanity.

The Reaper

1943,
Paris,
1990 dation

Ever since the beginning of the Thirties, in works like the *Woman with Leaves* of 1934, the inventive Picasso made figures which combined modeling and direct imprints of objects in fresh plaster. He used a cake mold for a head that looks as if it were crowned with a large straw hat, radiating like a sun, in the middle of which he added protuberances for the eyes, and incised a mouth to make a jolly-looking pastoral figure. The body, which was modeled in plaster, has a plantlike morphology: the arms and legs have incisions that recall branches or twisted vines. But the scythe peremptorily aimed at the ground suggests that this figure is not as inoffensive as it might seem, and may even be deceptive, another of the many hidden representations of Death in the artist's oeuvre, but here, with all the weight of a darkly-patinated bronze.

Man with a Sheep

February or March 1943,
Paris

A great number of drawings, executed since the month of July 1942, prepared the coming of this *Man with a Sheep* which Picasso, working in the large space of his studio of the rue des Grands-Augustins, modelled in wet clay in a single day; a plaster mold was made just as soon after, for the statue was in danger of crumbling under its own weight. Bronze casts were then made, one of which was given by the artist to the town of Vallauris and placed in its main square. Although this monumental figure belongs to the classical tradition in sculpture (the work of Rodin immediately comes to mind), Picasso did not hesitate to break the rules: certain parts are out of proportion to the whole (in particular the hands), the legs have only been modelled sketchily, the disposition of the volumes is not balanced (there is nothing in the stance of this strangely flat-footed figure that counterbalances the mass of the animal; this is particularly noticeable in a side view). This sta-

Man with a Sheep
Bronze
222.5 x 78 x 78 cm

The Reaper
Bronze
51 x 33.5 x 19.5 cm

tue naturally evokes the pastoral figures of Antiquity, or the Christian figure of the Good Shepherd, but Picasso strongly denied having had any symbolic intentions: "The man could just as well be carrying a pig instead of a sheep. There is nothing symbolic about it. It is beautiful, that's all."

Child with Doves
Oil on canvas
162 x 130 cm

Child with Doves

August 24, 1943,
Paris

A baby with a large head and round cheeks is seated on the floor in the shadows, holding a pacifier. "We called him Churchill, because of the resemblance", the painter once quipped. The wedge-shaped space seems constricted, oppressive, crushed by the weight of the black ceiling, but a bright ray of light, which projects the shadow of the chair on the wall, falls on the two white birds, symbols of hope during the dark days of the German occupation. These birds, a childhood memory (Picasso's father constantly painted pigeons, and his own first drawings as a child represented birds), were to appear more and more in his work, and would provide the motif for his world-famous image of the Dove of Peace.

Skull, Sea Urchins, and Lamp on a Table

November 27, 1946,
[Antibes or Paris]

The still life was one of the main themes of Picasso's paintings during the war. As if to make up for the food restrictions and shortages at the time, Picasso delighted in depicting tables covered with all manner of foods, fruit, vegetables, and fish. Often, these still lifes take on the melancholy cast of the "vanities", in which the objets represented are symbols of the frailty and futility of human endeavors in the face of inevitable death (a number of Picasso's friends had died recently, including Max Jacob and Robert Desnos, at Drancy and Terezin respectively, and Julio González, of a natural death). The skull is the most explicit of the symbols of mortality; the lamp, whose flame has gone out like the breath of life, is a reminder of the brief time given to each.

Skull, Sea Urchins, and Lamp
on a Table
Oil on plywood
81 x 100 cm

The sharply delineated forms, in a geometric style vaguely reminiscent of Cubism, and the stark contrast of the blacks, whites, and greys are perfectly suited to the somber mood of the picture. The sea urchins are the only reminders of the everyday reality of a happy summer spent at Antibes, working in the Palais Grimaldi.

The Kitchen

November 1948,
Paris

"I am going to make a painting of that, that is to say of nothing", Picasso proposed; the kitchen at the rue des Grands-Augustins was painted all in white, his companion Françoise Gilot later wrote, it was a sort of large cube in which the only spots of color

The Kitchen
Oil on canvas
175 x 252 cm

The She Goat
Plaster original
120.5 x 72 x 144 cm

were three Spanish plates hanging on the wall and some birds in their cage. Three round plates like targets, one of which is colored, and little birds that look as if they had been drawn by a child, are indeed visible among the tangle of black lines that cover the entire painting. The grey and white areas (some of them are not even painted, the white being that of the size used as a ground) that fit into or transgress this grid create forms that are independent of the lines and that make for what has been called a "flat depth". The long white form with a knob standing on the left side represents a door.

The She Goat

1950,
Vallauris

In the Thirties, in order to make sculptures, Picasso used to press all kinds of materials into his plaster; but here he used the objects themselves - bits and pieces of junk which the artist, a master scavenger, found at the Vallauris town dump -, setting them

directly into the plaster to make the animal; a slightly cropped palm frond for the back, an old wicker basket for the swollen belly (she is expecting), pieces of wood (with knots that look like joints) and metal for the legs, a twisted piece of metal for the tail; grapevine roots were used for the "goatee" and horns, cardboard for the ears, a tin can (that makes a hollow sound) for the sternum; two earthenware pots without their handles make the udder, a metal cover folded in half makes the sex organ, and a small piece of pipe the anus. Nothing is missing! This assemblage was then cast in bronze (also in the museum's collection), gaining in permanence to be sure, but to the detriment of the incomparable charm of the original materials.

Goat Skull, Bottle and Candle
Painted bronze
79 x 93 x 54 cm

Goat Skull and Bottle

1951-1953,
Vallauris

The original objects assembled with plaster to compose this sculpture have lost their identity somewhat in the bronze cast, but we can still easily make out the bicycle handlebars used for the horns of the goat, and the small nails for the curls bristling on the forehead; a piece of corrugated cardboard gave shape to the skull; long nails represent the rays of light of a candle stuck into the neck of the bottle. The masking of the original materials that resulted from the casting process was completed by the black and white paint (fitting colors for the somber theme of this still life subject often painted by Picasso during the war years): white paint was applied to the hollows of the corrugated texture and on other surfaces and edges, alternating with the black paint to create an oscillation between positive and negative, like in some photographs, that complicates our perception of the open form of the bottle (a procedure that Picasso used in the painted sculptures of the Cubist period).

Room 17 Picasso and Literature

Picasso's close ties with the world of literature were a constant feature of his long career: as an intimate of writers and poets, he illustrated their books, while they in turn sang his praises in their writings. What's more - and this is perhaps the least-known aspect of his art - Picasso himself wrote: the painter was also a poet. A vast quantity of documents, manuscripts, letters, photographs, magazines, illustrated books, engraved plates, and portraits bear witness to this fruitful encounter between the worlds of the letters and of the arts. The Picasso archives, which complete the collections of the museum, constitute a wealth of source material in this field.

Picasso's first friends in Paris at the beginning of the century were poets: Max Jacob and André Salmon, whose books he illustrated with his plates: Salmon's *Poèmes* in 1905, Max Jacob's *Saint Matorel*, in 1911, and *Le Siège de Jérusalem* in 1914, among other works. He was very close to Guillaume Apollinaire, who became the fervent defender of Cubism in his *Méditations Esthétiques*, published in 1913. He met Pierre Reverdy in 1910, illustrating his *Cravates de chanvre* in 1922, and *Le Chant des morts* in 1948 (of which the museum owns the original maquette).

Picasso's encounter with Jean Cocteau in 1915 was the beginning of his great adventure with the Ballets Russes and of a long friendship celebrated in the latter's *L'Ode à Picasso, poème 1917*, and in a small monograph published in 1922, which cooled somewhat during the war years and was resumed afterwards. In 1918 he made the acquaintance of André Breton and the group of Surrealist writers around him: Benjamin Péret, Georges Hugnet, Louis Aragon, Paul Eluard (who became a life-long friend and collaborator: in 1936 Picasso illustrated Eluard's *La Barre d'appui* and *Les Yeux fertiles*, in 1944 *Au Rendez-vous allemand*, in 1945 *A Pablo Picasso*). From this period also dates his meeting with René Char. The leading magazines of literature and the arts that came out in the Thirties published some fundamental texts on the painter's work: Breton wrote at length about Picasso in "Le surréalisme et la peinture", printed in *La Révolution surréaliste* in 1925, and the admirable text "Picasso dans son élément" in the first issue of *Minotaure*, in 1933. Exhibition catalogues were the occasion for memorable prefaces, such as Aragon's "La peinture au défi" for the exhibition of collages at the Galerie Goemans in 1930. Others linked with the Surrealist period were Georges Bataille and Michel Leiris, whose friendship with Picasso lasted to the very end.

Sur le dos de l'immence [sic] tranche
de melon ardent
Poem, December 14, 1935
India ink and colored pencil
25.5 x 17.1 cm

The postwar period brought with it new poets, and new books to illustrate: those of Pierre André Benoit (who was also a publisher), Iliazd, Jacques Prévert.

"Picasso poète", with this title André Breton revealed in his *Cahiers d'art* of 1936 the hidden side of an already protean production. Picasso turned to writing in 1935, at a time when he was so beset by problems in his personal life that he was unable to paint. He covered entire notebooks with unpunctuated texts, prose poems in Spanish and in French (he wrote constantly, and anywhere, even, as Sabartés tells us, sitting on the edge of his bathtub), texts transcribed on drawing paper, manuscripts in a very careful hand - the handwriting of a painter - "illuminated" by his corrections, or inkspots that he improvised with, or efflorescences as the ink seeped into the paper. These texts were sometimes accompanied by elaborate drawings (pen and ink portraits of Marie-Thérèse in 1936). The collection of the museum consists principally of a set of manuscripts from 1936, most of which are unpublished, a notebook dating from his sojourn in Royan at the beginning of the war, and the manuscript of a play written in 1952, *Les Quatre Petites Filles*.

Room 18 Vallauris

1947-1954

1947	May 15	Birth of Claude, son of Picasso and Françoise Gilot.
	Summer	Picasso begins to make ceramics at Vallauris.
1948	Summer	Picasso and Françoise move into the villa *La Galloise* in Vallauris.
1949	April 19	Birth of Paloma, daughter of Picasso and Françoise.
1950		Sculpture predominates in his work.
	June 25	Beginning of the Korean War.
1952	November 18	Death of Paul Eluard.
1953	Autumn	Deterioration of Picasso's relationship with Françoise, who moves back to Paris with her children.
1954	June	Two portraits of "Madame Z" announce the presence of a new woman in Picasso's life: Jacqueline Roque.
	November 3	Death of Matisse.

Françoise Gilot and Picasso
at La Galloise,
Vallauris, 1952
(Documentation
du musée Picasso,
photo: R. Doisneau)

Woman in an Armchair
Oil and gouache on canvas
130.2 x 97.1 cm

Woman in an Armchair

July 3, 1946,
Paris

Françoise Gilot, Picasso's new companion, is a beautiful young woman with a slender waist and an abundant head of hair. One of the most specific features of her face is the eyebrow that arches above her right eye. Once again, as in the case of the portraits of Marie-Thérèse, the particularities of the model's anatomy led the painter to a characteristic representation: he accentuated the slenderness of the body, of the neck, and the narrowness of the waist; increased the volume of the breasts and of the hair, which becomes like a crown of petals around the small round head. If, for Picasso, Marie-Thérèse was the woman who sleeps, and Dora Maar the woman who weeps, Françoise was the flower-woman, because of her plantlike vivacity; a vision that he materialized in a painting which so moved him that he said he would repeat it "*à l'infini*".

Girl Jumping Rope

1950,
Vallauris

To make a weightless sculpture, one that did not touch the ground, boldly negating the requirements of sculpture, this had been one of Picasso's dreams. And this is just what he achieved here, depicting the little girl jumping up as her rope touches the ground. The rope - a bent metal bar - is what holds the entire sculpture; yet another example of Picasso's magical ability to materialize the "mysterious truth of life", as J. Leymarie put it, through the ingenious transposition of the most banal and unexpected objects. The imprint of the round cover of a chocolate box made the face, which is framed by hair made by the impression of a piece of corrugated cardboard; the two little ears were the handles of a ceramic pot. A shallow wicker basket made the bust; metal bars hold the skirt, whose shape was cast with newspapers; the short wooden legs have oversized feet wearing unmatching shoes found in a junkyard. There is a flower growing nearby, made

Girl Jumping Rope
Plaster original
152 x 65 x 66 cm

Pregnant Woman
Bronze
109 x 30 x 34 cm

with cookie molds and a hot-plate, and also a snake. This touching and humorous figure is a perfect image of childhood: a well-groomed little girl, who looks very proper, blithely skipping rope, her skims flying; in play, she has put on shoes that are too big for her feet.

Pregnant Woman

1950-1959,
Vallauris

In 1947 Françoise gave birth to Claude, and in 1949 to Paloma, hence the reappearance of the theme of motherhood in Picasso's work at this time. The figure here is vigorous and hieratic, set firmly on its legs, square-shouldered, arms held at the sides, proudly carrying its swollen breasts and a prominent belly that is perpendicular to the straight back (the round and smooth forms of the breasts and belly were given by ceramic jars that Picasso incorporated into the original sculpture before it was cast in bronze, thus materializing the traditional

metaphor which compares woman to a vessel). Françoise, the model, did not much like this sculpture in which she saw "the image of a woman only just evolved from the ape", and which she found "pathetic" and "grotesque", yet which nonetheless has some of the coarse beauty of an archaic fertility goddess.

Massacre in Korea

January 18, 1951,
Vallauris

More than once in his career, Picasso felt the need to express his political involvement through his painting. But he always did so in his own terms, provoking each time reactions of surprise, if not incomprehension and disapprobation, from the political activists who were counting on his involvement. When he painted *Guernica* in 1937, he was reproached with not having represented the massacre realistically enough. Matters did not improve - far from it - when he joined the Communist Party in

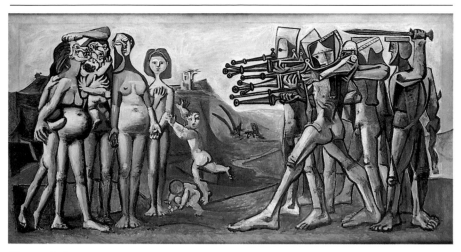

Massacre in Korea
Oil on plywood
110 x 210 cm

1944, since he was not about to "toe the line", that is, to submit to the official aesthetic doctrine of the Party, which at the time preached Socialist Realism. And yet a painting like the *Massacre in Korea* stands as a testimonial to Picasso's good faith: the subject - soldiers executing defenseless women and children - could be read as a denunciation of the American intervention in Korea. But the manner was not quite right, the canvas was poorly received at the Salon de Mai; and so Picasso's work had been for nothing. When, at the death of Stalin, the Communist newspaper *Les Lettres françaises* printed Picasso's portrait of the Soviet leader (represented as a young man in a rather "rough-hewn" drawing), the Party officially expressed its disapprobation; Picasso was reproached with not painting like the more orthodox Fougeron.

Baboon and Young

October 1951,
Vallauris

Two small toy cars, a present from Kahnweiler to the little Claude, a Panhard and a Renault, placed chassis to chassis, then two little plaster balls in the windshield of the Panhard, and ceramic jar handles for the ears: what could look more like the head of a baboon! Picasso again combined several techniques: modelling, imprints, assemblage; plaster molded in a basin and striated with a knife made the furry neck, a large terracotta jug gave shape to the animal's body, the handles becoming its shoulders, ceramic stands (usually used to support and arrange pottery in the kiln for firing) were used as the core for the plaster legs, and a bent metal slat, from a door or a shutter, became the tail.

Baboon and Young
Plaster original
56 x 34 x 71 cm

Jacqueline with Crossed Hands
Oil on canvas
116 x 88.5 cm

Jacqueline
with Crossed Hands

June 3, 1954,
Vallauris
1990 dation

June 3, 1954. The portrait of a young woman seated on the floor, with tightly intertwined fingers gathering her knees against her body, barred by the thick yellow stripes of the skirt, from which protrude two bare feet planted firmly on the ground. On top of a disproportionately long neck perches a proud head crowned by a helmet of hair. Picasso put this formidable "modern sphinx" - as Antonina Vallentin called her - in richly-colored surroundings, to which he gave depth by scratching the lines of the floor directly into the paint. The title of this first portrait, "Madame Z...", did not reveal the model's identity. The secret, however, did not remain one for long, and Jacqueline Roque became the painter's companion and wife until the very end, ma-

nifesting her constant presence in his work. In this portrait of his beloved, who was modest and reserved according to those who knew her, Picasso showed that he had sensed her passionate pride and stubbornness. And probably also, from the very beginning, her striking resemblance to the woman with a water pipe seated on the right in Delacroix's *Les Femmes d'Alger*, a picture of which he would soon be painting many interpretations thanks to the stimulus of his living model.

Room **19** Cannes Vauvenargues

1955-1961

1955	February 11	Death of Olga Picasso.
	June-October	Retrospective exhibition at the Musée des Arts Décoratifs in Paris.
	Summer	Clouzot makes the film *Le Mystère Picasso*.
1958	January	Completes a mural project for the UNESCO building in Paris: *The Fall of Icarus*, installed in September.
	September	Picasso buys the Château de Vauvenargues that stands at the foot of the Montagne Sainte-Victoire, near Aix-en-Provence, and establishes himself there in the following year.
1959	September 19	Inauguration of chapel in Vallauris for which Picasso painted a mural on the theme of War and Peace.
1961	March 2	Picasso and Jacqueline Roque marry in Vallauris.

Picasso and Jacqueline at La Californie
(Archives Picasso, photo D.D. Duncan)

The Studio at La Californie

March 30, 1956,
Cannes

We are at La Californie, a spacious 19th-century villa overlooking Cannes to which Picasso moved in 1955, and more exactly in one of the vast ground-floor rooms whose large, decorative windows look out onto a luxuriant garden (here, some have their shutters closed). This is where the painter set up his studio, filling it with his works and familiar objects; a Moroccan brazier, a cupboard, a stool. There is no human presence here: the studio looks like a theater stage set for the performance of Art. There is a little sculpture, recognizable by its lozenge-shaped head, and a painting, the only colorful passage here, which can be identified as a portrait of Jacqueline in a Turkish costume. Picasso painted many such "inner landscapes", which he also called "interior landscapes"; this one is very Spanish in its austerity ("Velázquez", prompts Picasso), with its somber tonality, and play of light and dark. Practically in the middle stands an easel with a blank canvas, which is exactly what it is, for the white is in fact the sized, unpainted canvas itself. This deserted, somewhat eerie place might well be haunted by the spirit of Matisse, Picasso's great rival, who had died two years before and who invariably comes to mind here when we consider this picture's subject - a studio that is very Matisse-like in its tidiness and the manner in which it was handled - all in arabesques and fluid colors.

The Bathers

1956,
Cannes

Picasso assembled pieces of wood of all kinds (boards or manufactured objects that are easily recognizable in the bronze cast) to construct this monumental group of six bathers which he situated in their projected contexts in drawings during the autumn of that year: the scene takes place at the seashore, the woman diver (the tallest of the figures: with arms made from broom handles, and feet from those of a bed) and the man with joined hands (the arms were made from a picture frame) are on a jetty; the woman with outstretched, flailing arms and the young man are on the diving-board; the fountain-man and the child, whose upper body only is visible, are in the water. Anatomical details have been incised into the wood: faces, chest muscles, genitals, legs. These flat sculptures were made to be seen frontally.

The Studio at La Californie
Oil on canvas
114 x 146 cm

The Bathers
Bronze
Between 136 and 228 cm high

Le déjeuner sur l'herbe, after Manet
Oil on canvas
130 x 195 cm

Le Déjeuner sur l'herbe, after Manet

March 3 - August 20, 1960,
Vauvenargues

Picasso was not afraid to confront his art to that of the great masters of European painting, and it would even seem that this became for him a vital necessity, inspiring him to choose as themes for his many variations: the *Crucifixion* of Grünewald, Courbet's *Women on the Banks of the Seine*, Delacroix's *Women of Algiers*, Velázquez's *The Maids of Honor* (*Las Meninas*)... and here, Manet's *Luncheon on the Grass*. Between 1956 and 1961, through a large number of paintings (four of which are in the museum), more than a hundred drawings, and even small cardboard maquettes (from which monumental concrete sculptures were made for the garden of the Modema Museet in Stockholm), Picasso undertook an impressive stylistic exercise, subjecting this composition to an unending variety of interpretations. Here the figures are disposed in about the same way as in Manet's work: on the right, the "talker" with his cane and black coat, and facing him, the seated nude (these two figures also evoke

the perennial couple of the painter and his model); standing behind the seated woman is the other man, dressed in brown and lost in the scenery (in Manet's painting he is sitting); in the back, merging with the water and greenery, is the dislocated figure of the woman who is bathing. Picasso had many reasons for turning to the art of former masters; there is no doubt that he wanted to make sure that his work could stand up to that of his predecessors (he took the opportunity of doing so in 1948, when he asked that the works he had just donated to the Musée National d'Art Moderne be taken the Louvre and placed next to works by Zurbarán, Delacroix, Courbet, and Uccello, so that he could see for himself). It may be, too, that he wanted to show that the works of others could be approached like any other subject and interpreted completely differently, and thus be given a new life through new eyes and hands (yet some took this as a decline, a sign that he had run out of subjects).

Metal Cutouts

1961

Often in the past, Picasso had cut out, folded, and painted pieces of sheet metal to create objects: in 1915, a violin; in 1924, a guitar. It was in Vallauris, at the beginning of the Sixties, while visiting a factory specialized in the folding of metal, that he glimpsed the creative potential in a collaboration between artist and technician. The sculptor had only to cut out paper to make a model, the shapes and folds (sometimes quite complex, as in the *Seated Pierrot*) creating shadows that defined the volume. From this model, full-scale versions (sometimes in several copies) could then be faithfully reproduced in the factory, using more or less thick sheets of metal. Works in paper, - which is so marvellously pliable in the artist's hands, but so limited because of its fragility -, could thus be given a stable and durable form. The metal was then painted, generally in white, but sometimes in color, or touched up with crayons (like the *Footballers*). The most amazing of these sculptures is perhaps *The Chair*, which, in Picasso's words, looks like "a chair that's been under a steamroller", and then bent back into shape to stand on its legs.

The Chair
Cut, folded, and painted sheet metal
111.5 x 114.5 x 89 cm

Seated Pierrot
Cut, folded, assembled,
and painted sheet metal
134.5 x 57 x 57 cm

Room **20** Mougins: The Last Years

1961-1973

1961	June	Picasso and Jacqueline move to the villa Notre-Dame-de-Vie at Mougins.
1962		For the next ten years Picasso will work intensively on engraving.
1963	March	Opening of the Picasso Museum in Barcelona.
	August 31	Death of Braque.
1964		Publication of Françoise Gilot's book, *Life with Picasso*, and of Brassaï's Conversations avec *Picasso*.
1966	November	Large retrospective "Hommage à Picasso" in Paris (organized by J. Leymarie); seven hundred works exhibited (the sculpture came as a revelation).
1968	February 13	Death of Sabartés; in his memory, Picasso donates a series of paintings on the theme of *Las Meninas* to the Museo Picasso in Barcelona.
1970	Summer	Exhibition of recent works at the palais des Papes in Avignon (organized by Yvonne and Christian Zervos).
1971	October 25	In honor of Picasso's 90th birthday, a selection of his works are displayed in the Grande Galerie of the Louvre.
1973	April 8	Picasso dies at the villa Notre-Dame-de-Vie. He is buried at Vauvenargues on April 10.

Woman with Outstretched Arms

1961,
Cannes

It all began with a sheet of paper torn out of a pad with a spiral binding: the paper was simply cut and folded to make the 30-centimeter-high figure of a woman standing up with outstretched arms (the perforated fringe of the paper torn from the binding made the fingers of one hand). From an enlargement of this model, Picasso had a metal sheet cut out, then folded and painted in white. Metal wire or wire grating was used to outline or cover the parts painted in black: features of the face, navel, pubic triangle, fingers and toes, and the shadows around the head and one of the arms. This sculpture was two meters high, and the story does not end there, for it was to be enlarged to monumental dimensions (in keeping with one of Picasso's long-standing preoccupations); in 1962, Carl Nesjar raised a 6-meter-high version of this female figure - which was called *The Angel* - in the garden of Kahnweiler estate at Saint-Hilaire, in the Essonne region. The Norwegian sculptor had perfected a technique for casting the sculpture in concrete and then sandblasting it to bring out the texture of the stones in the concrete mixture; several large sculptures were executed in this way after models provided by Picasso.

Woman with Outstretched Arms
Cut, folded, and painted sheet metal, painted wire grating
183 x 177.5 x 72.5 cm

Woman with Pillow

July 10,
1969

The history of painting is marked by a number of admirable nudes, glorious celebrations of the female body - Venus and Danaë by Titian, Velásquez and Rembrandt - or odalisques and ordinary nudes when the pretext was no longer mythological; Goya, Ingres, Matisse, etc. This *Woman with Pillow*, a monumental woman with nacreous flesh whose pose naturally recalls Goya's *Maja Desnuda*, belongs to a long classical tradition. The body was drawn with a thick, black outline that respects the model's anatomy, set against the white of the canvas, which was left largely unpainted. Only the face presents the morphology characteristic of Picasso, combining frontal and profile views - one eye being shown frontally, the other in profile, and the nose in profile with both nostrils visible - the two aspects seeming to be kissing tenderly where the lips meet. An ivory-colored layer of paint partially covers with a same glow the smoothness of the skin and the softness of the sheet. To quote Baudelaire: "There, all is beauty and order/Luxury, calm and pleasure."

The Kiss

October 26, 1969,
Mougins

Almost half a century had gone by since Picasso painted same subject (1925) at Juan-les-Pins, but it seems that his desire was just as strong as ever. In the last years of his life, Picasso represented scenes of lovemaking with an unprecedented urgency: was it just an elderly man's obsession (he was 88 years old), or was it the affirmation of the thing that - along with painting - gave meaning to his life? The two ultimate themes of his work are indeed love and painting. In this

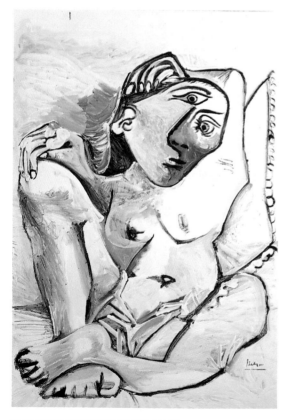

Woman with Pillow
Oil on canvas
194 x 130 cm

Room 20

The Kiss
Oil on canvas
97 x 130 cm

embrace, the two faces are pressed toge-ther, their fleshy forms meet, merge, blend, the nostrils dilated, the lips full. The lovers are completely absorbed with their kissing, they look literally shaken, but they keep their eyes open.

Seated Old Man

September 26, 1970 - November 14, 1971, Mougins

The pose of the gardener Vallier painted by Cézanne, the straw hat of Van Gogh, the puffy, embroidered sleeve of the colorful Rumanian blouse painted by Matisse, the paralyzed, arthritic hand of Renoir at the

Seated Old Man
Oil on canvas
145.5. x 114 cm

The Matador
Oil on canvas
145.5 x 114 cm

end of his life; this bearded old man seated in a wicker armchair (whose rounded back becomes a sleeve) secretly condenses, and reveals to the initiated, allusions and a form of homage (deliberate or unconscious?) to the great masters of the recent century. A dazzling yet pathetic image, for even with its bright colors and brisk execution, one can sense that life is coming undone: the stump of the hand shows that the body is afflicted, the dripping paint smudges the features of the face, the blankly staring eyes have the clouded iris of the aged.

mely vivid contrasts (oranges and blues); the execution is brisk, almost feverish, for time was short and the painter still had much to say. It was as if, day by day, an unbelievable energy, a generous flow of life kept guiding the pencil, brush, or burin in Picasso's hand. We can almost hear him whispering to himself, "I'm hurrying, I'm hurrying as fast as I can…".

The Matador

October 4, 1970,
Mougins

A host of baroque and fantastic figures crowded into one: musketeers, melon-eaters, smokers, toreros. The matador (identifiable by the net around his hair) smoking a big cigar here is also a gentleman, the descendant of those painted by Velázquez and Rembrandt, with their ruffled lace collars and sleeves. The pigments are thick and bright, applied in many layers, with extre-

Brief bibliography

General works:

Brassaï
Picasso & Co.
London and New York, 1967.

Cabanne, Pierre
Le Siècle de Picasso, Paris, Gallimard,
collection Folio-essais, 1992.

Daix, Pierre
La vie de peintre de Pablo Picasso, Paris,
édition du Seuil, 1977.
Picasso créateur, la vie intime et l'œuvre,
Paris, Seuil, 1987.

Fermigier, André
Picasso, Paris, Le Livre de Poche, 1969.

Malraux, André
La Tête d'obsidienne, Paris, Gallimard,
1974.

Penrose, Roland
Picasso, re. ed. Harmondsworth and New
York, 1971.

Richardson, John, with the collaboration
of Marilyn McCully,
Vie de Picasso, vol. 1 (1981-1906), Paris,
Editions du Chêne, 1992 (vol. 2 still to be
published).

**Works dealing specifically with the
collection of the Musée Picasso:**

Besnard-Bernadac, Marie-Laure
Musée Picasso, les chefs-d'œuvre
Paris, Editions de la Réunion des musées
nationaux – Prestel, 1991.

Musée Picasso. Catalogue sommaire des
collections, t. I (peintures, papiers collés,
sculptures, céramiques), Paris, Editions de
la Réunion des Musées nationaux, 1985.

Musée Picasso. Catalogue sommaire des
collections, t. II (dessins, aquarelles,
gouaches, pastels), Paris, Editions de la
Réunion des Musées nationaux, 1987.

Musée Picasso. Carnets. Catalogue des
dessins, vols. I & II, Paris, Editions de la
Réunion des musées nationaux, 1996.

Picasso, une nouvelle dation, Paris,
Editions de la Réunion des Musées
nationaux, 1990.

and on the Hôtel Salé:

Musée Picasso, l'hôtel Salé, coll. Petits
guides des grands musées, Paris, Editions
de la Réunion des musées nationaux, 1985.

Musée Picasso, les collections, coll. Petits
guides des grands musées, Paris, Editions
de la Réunion des musées nationaux, 1991.

Babelon, Jean-Pierre, "La maison du
bourgeois gentilhomme: l'hôtel Salé, 5,
rue de Thorigny à Paris", Revue de l'art,
n° 68, Paris, June 1985.

Foucart, Bruno, "De l'hôtel Salé au musée
Picasso", Revue de l'art, n° 68, Paris, June
1985.

Photo Credits: Réunion des musées nationaux (unless indicated otherwise)

This book was printed in december 2001, on the presses of Aubin, Ligugé.
The illustrations were engraved by Clair Offset, Gentilly.
Lay-out by Bruno Pfäffli

1er Dépôt légal août 1996
Dépôt légal décembre 2001
ISBN 2-7118-3532-4
GG 20 3532